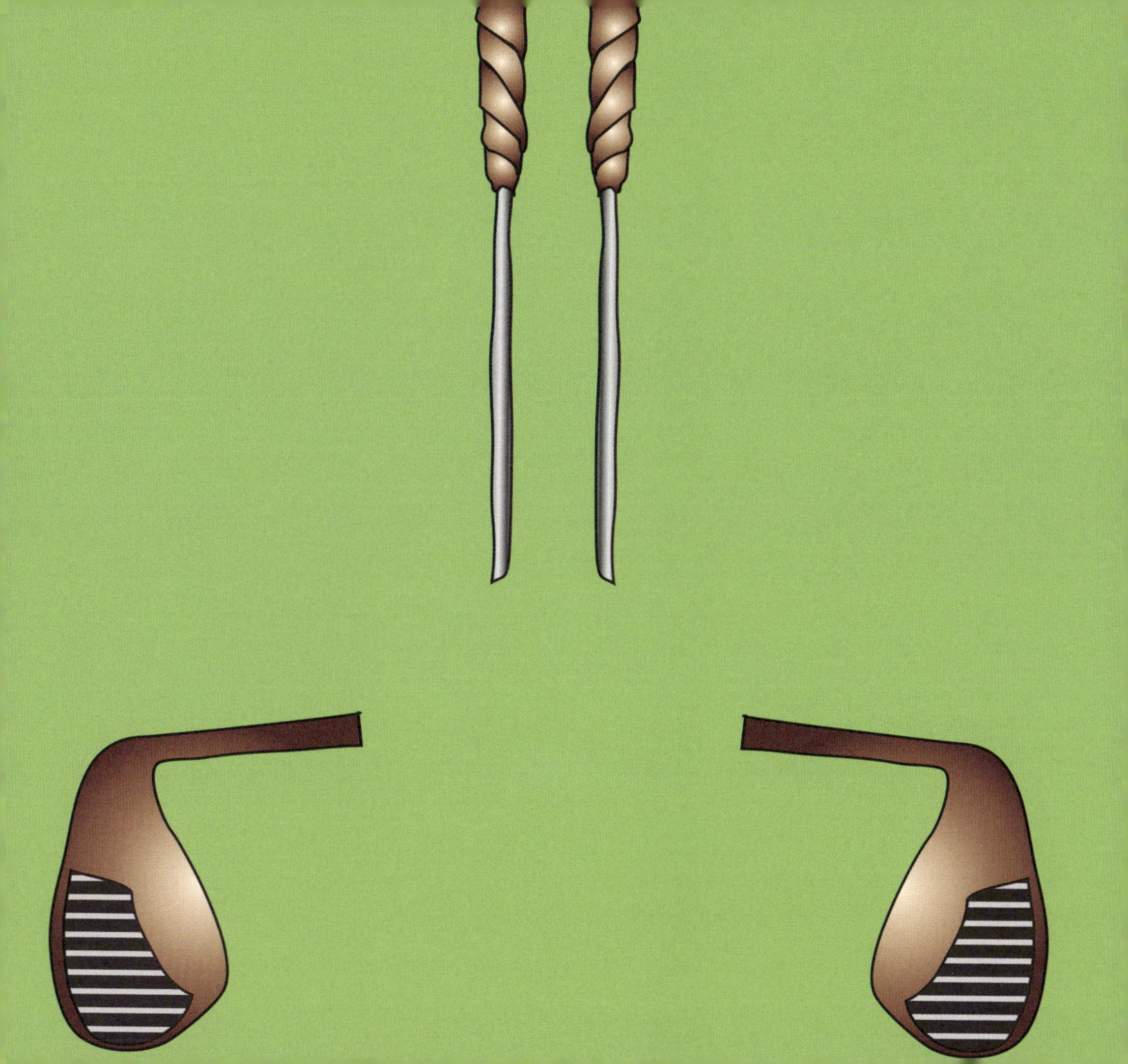

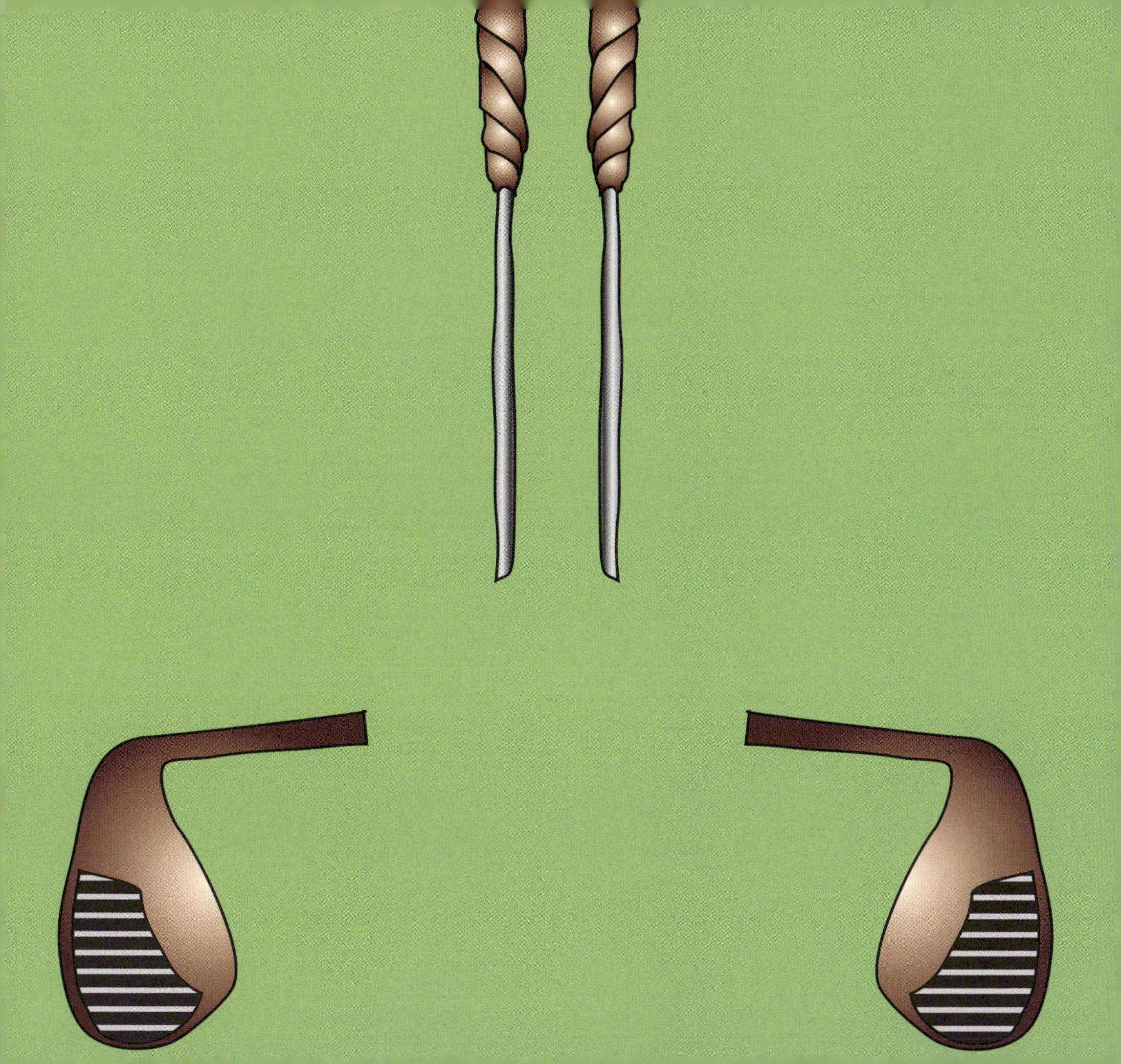

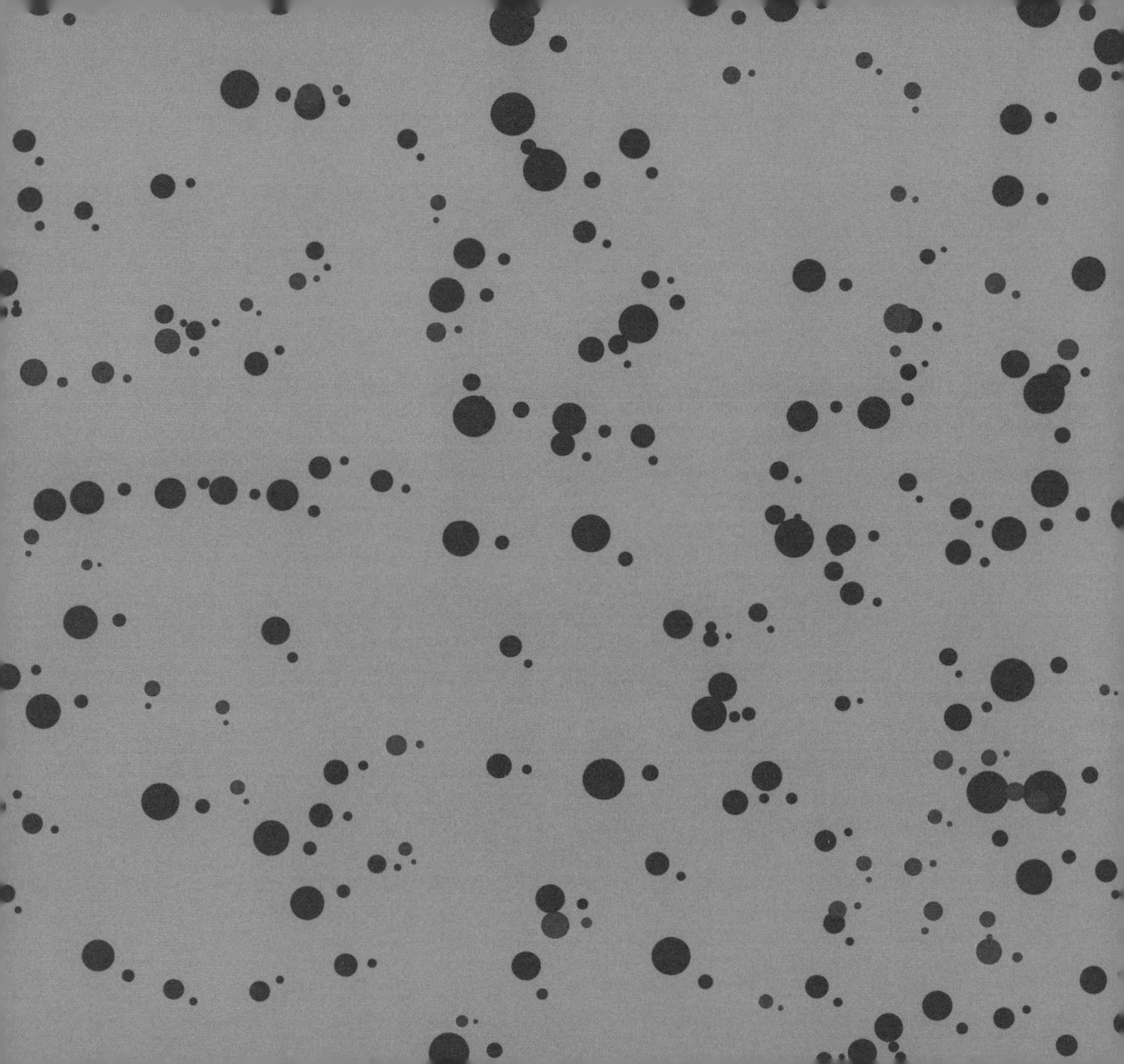

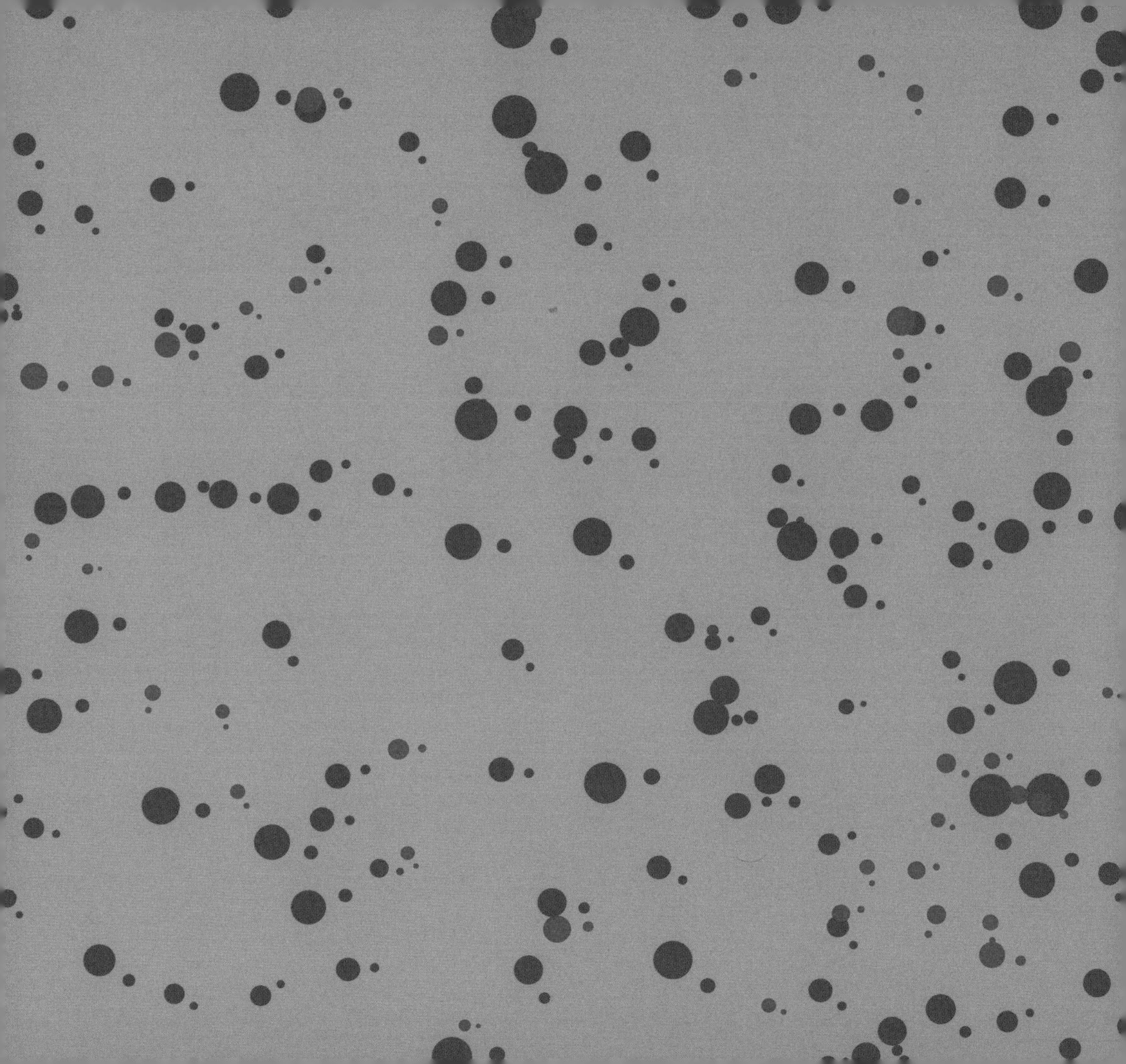

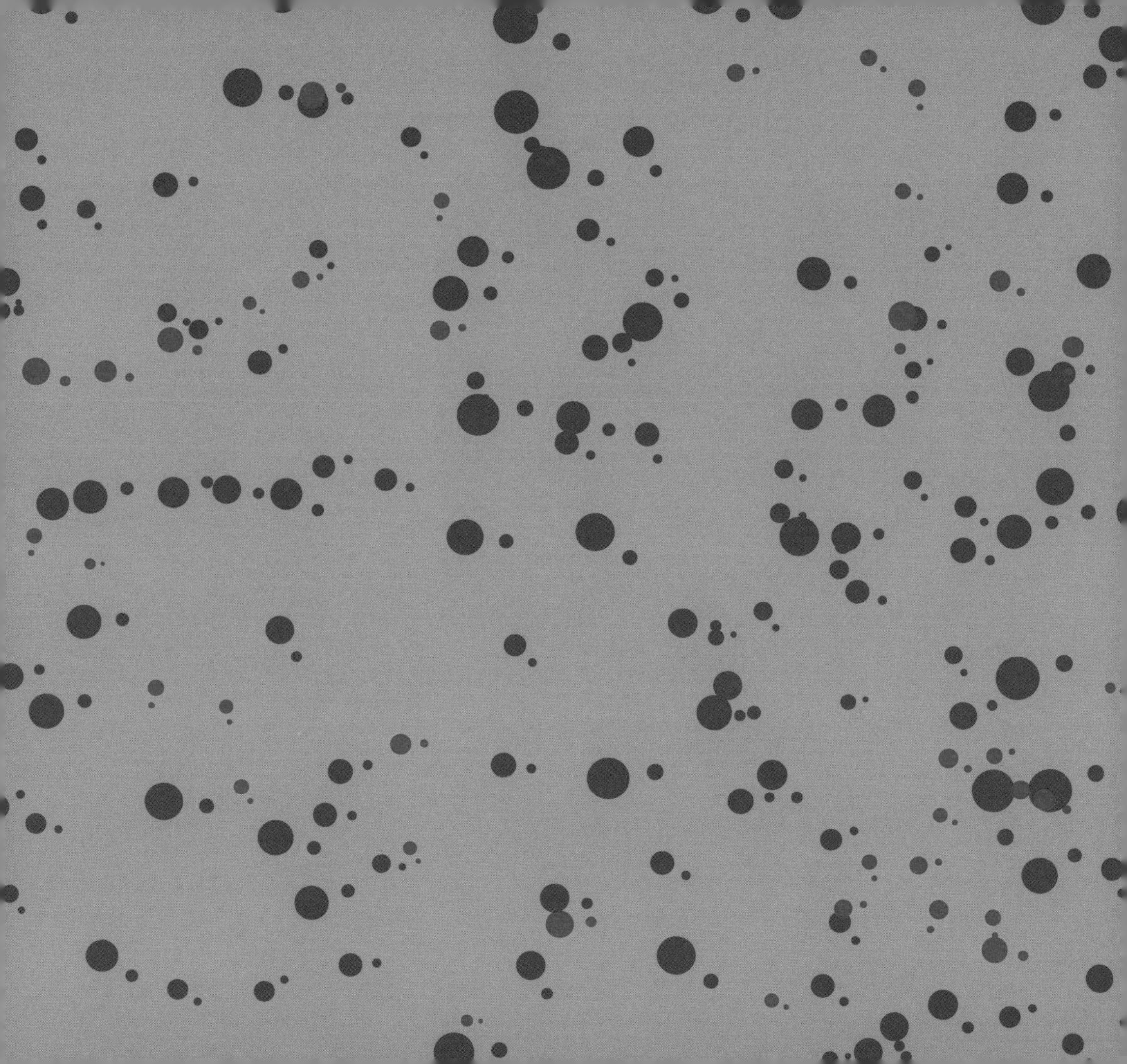

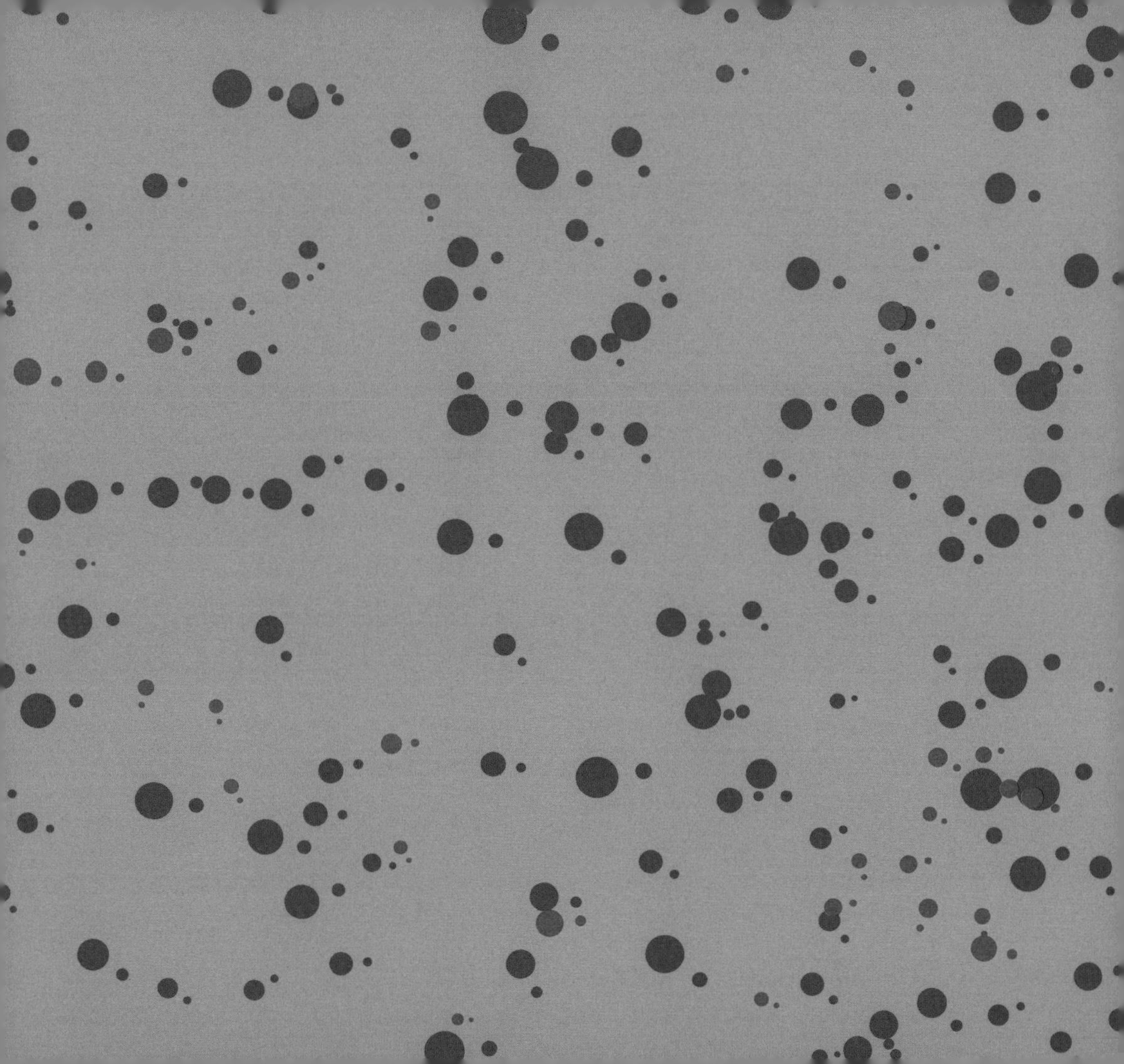

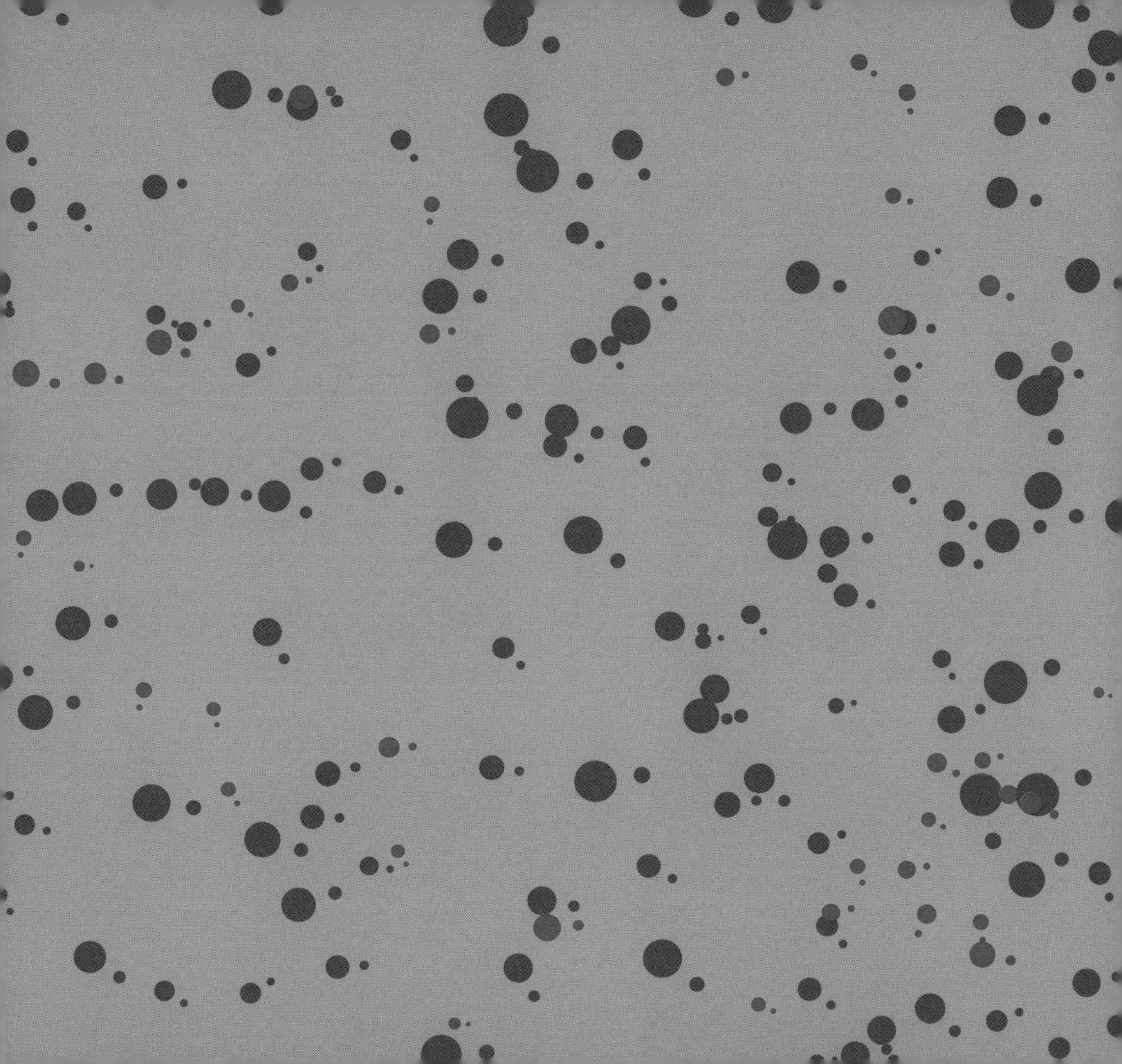

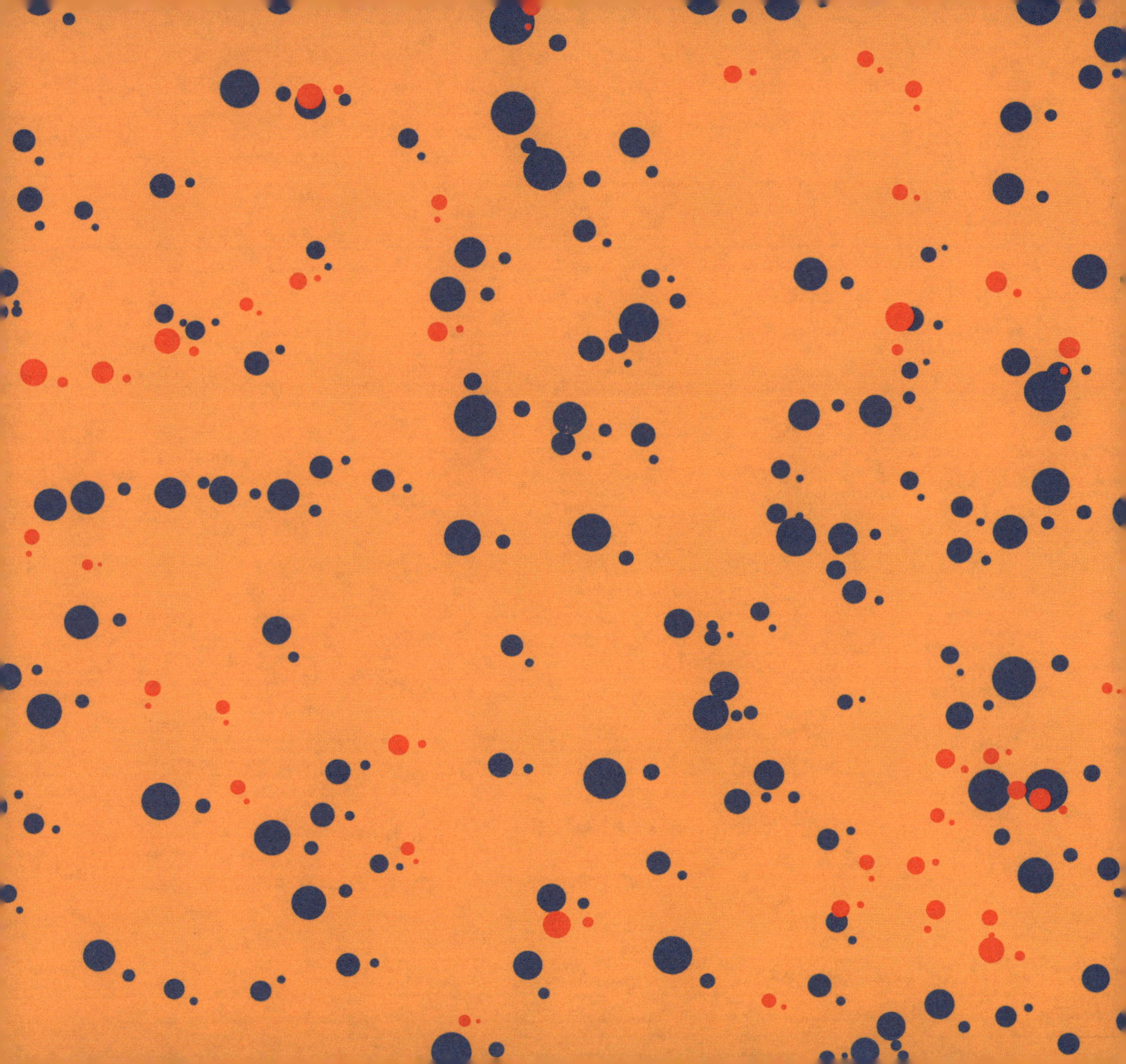

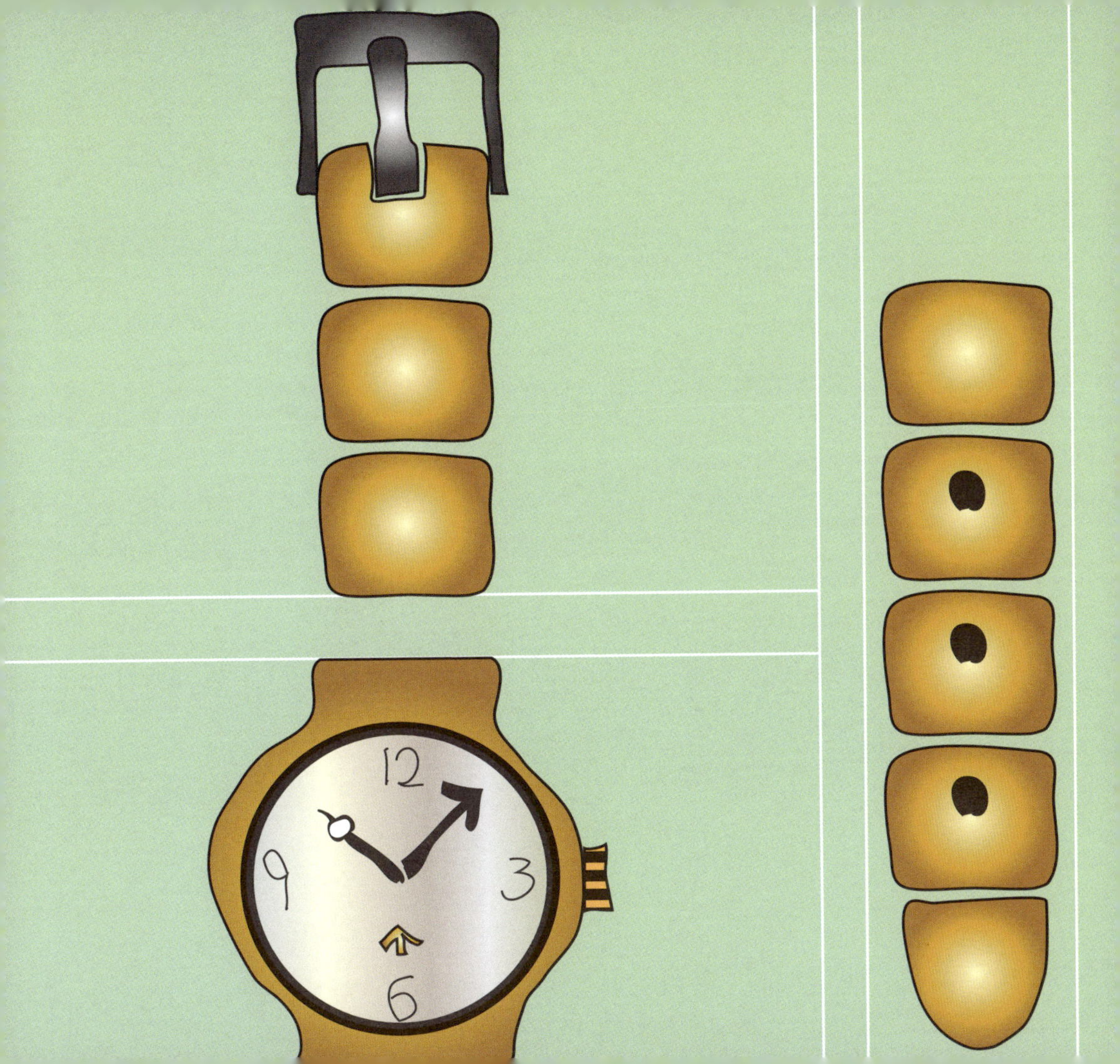
12
9
3
6

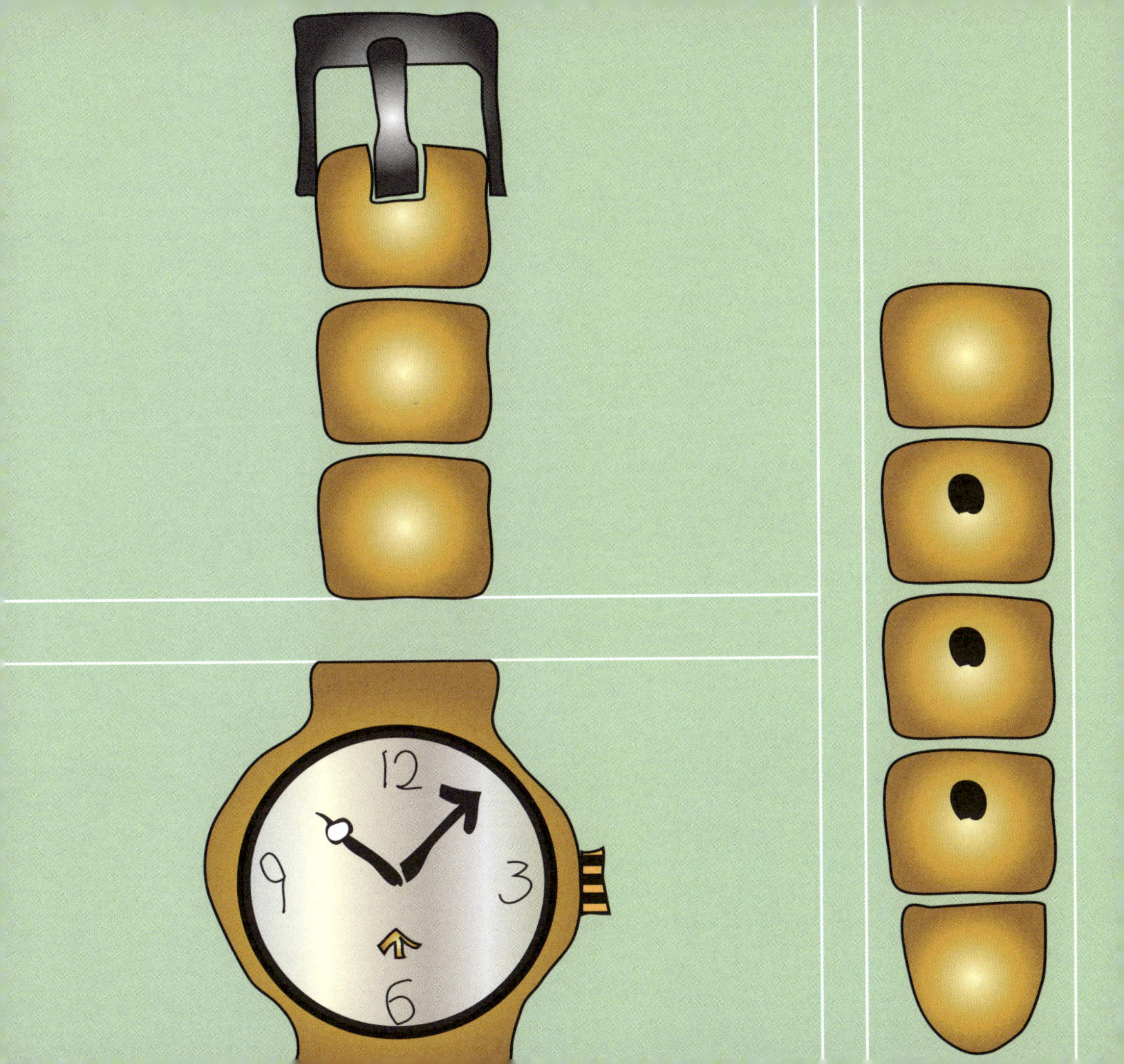
12
9
3
6

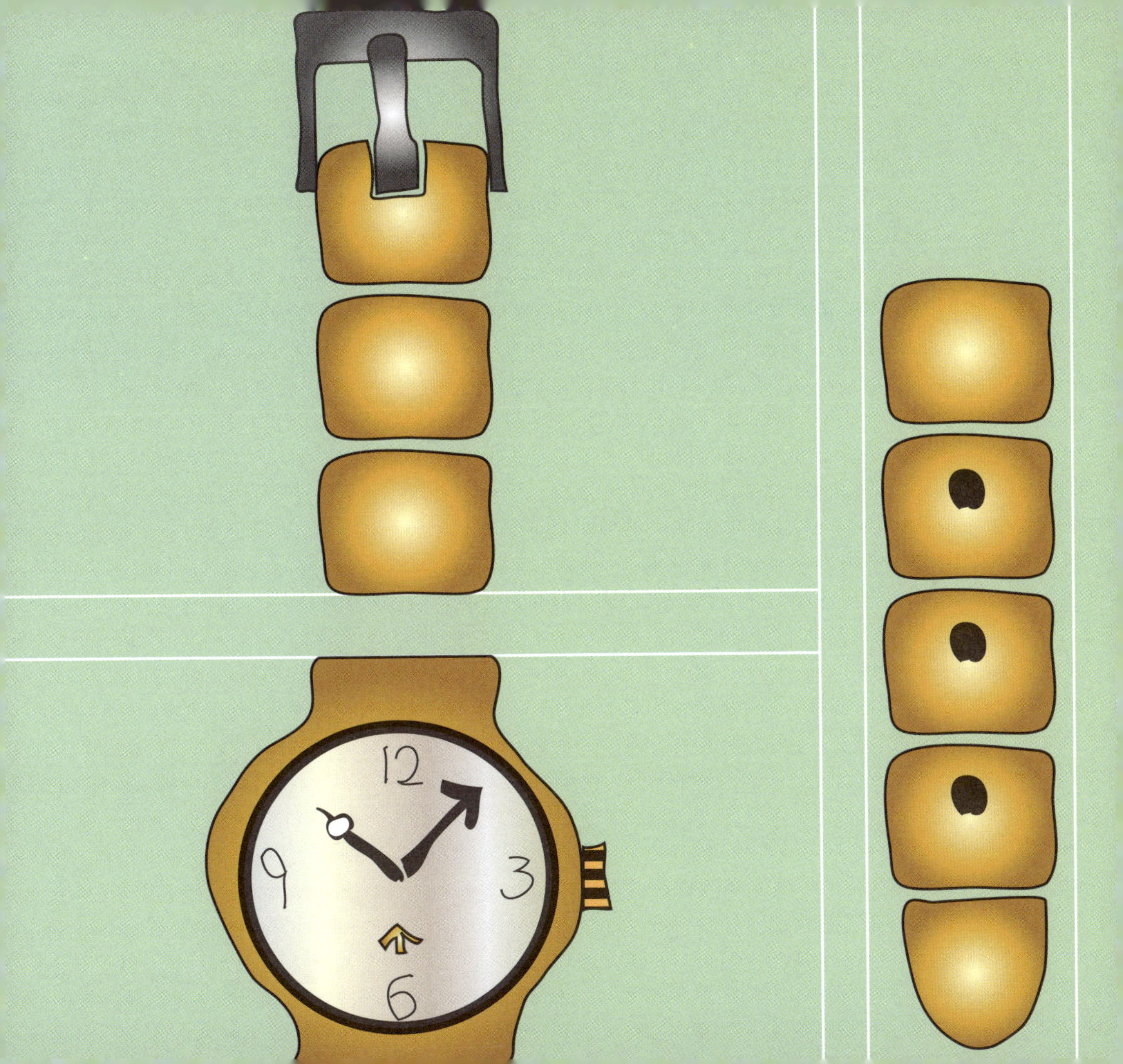
12
3
6
9

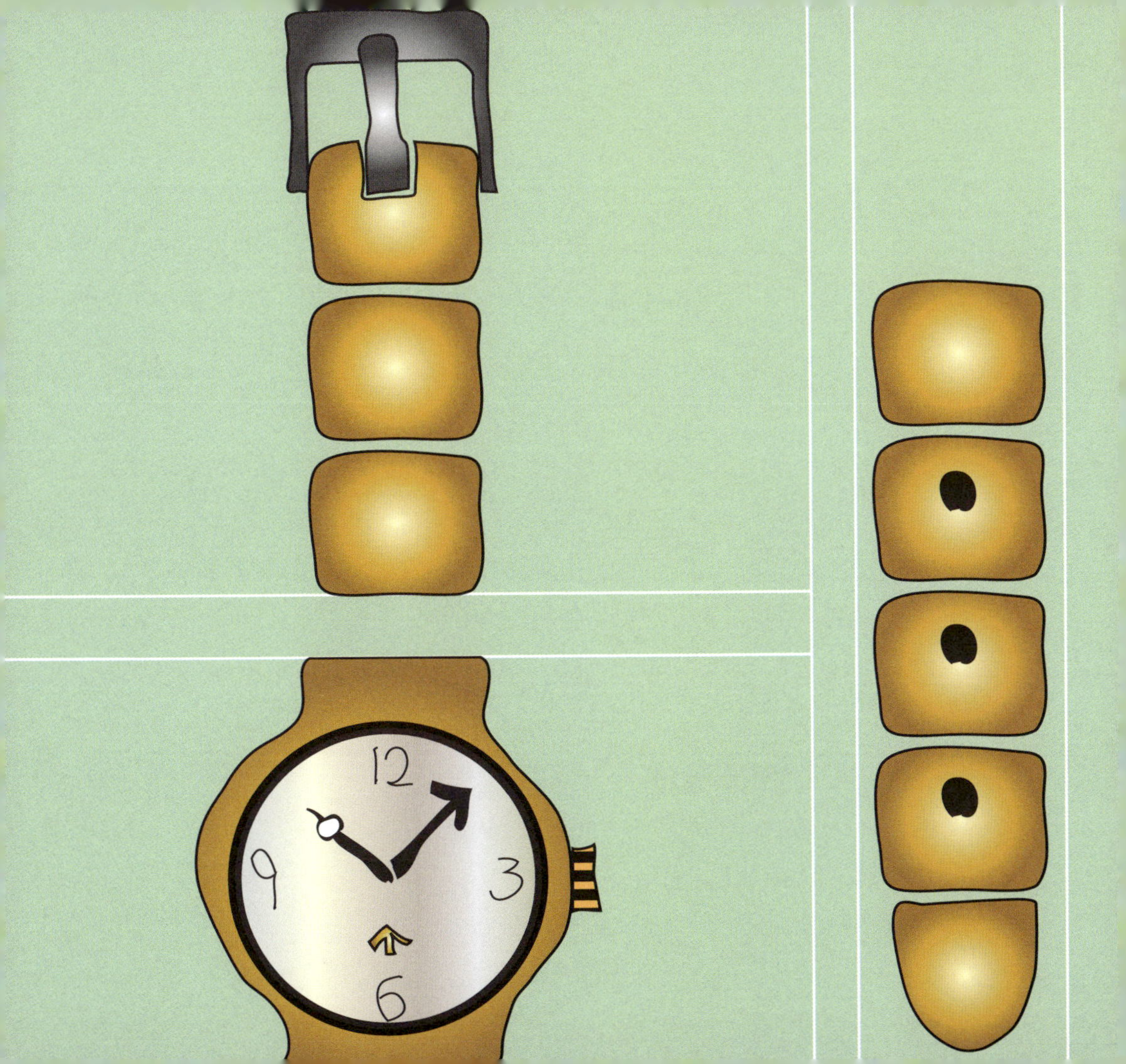
12
9
3
6

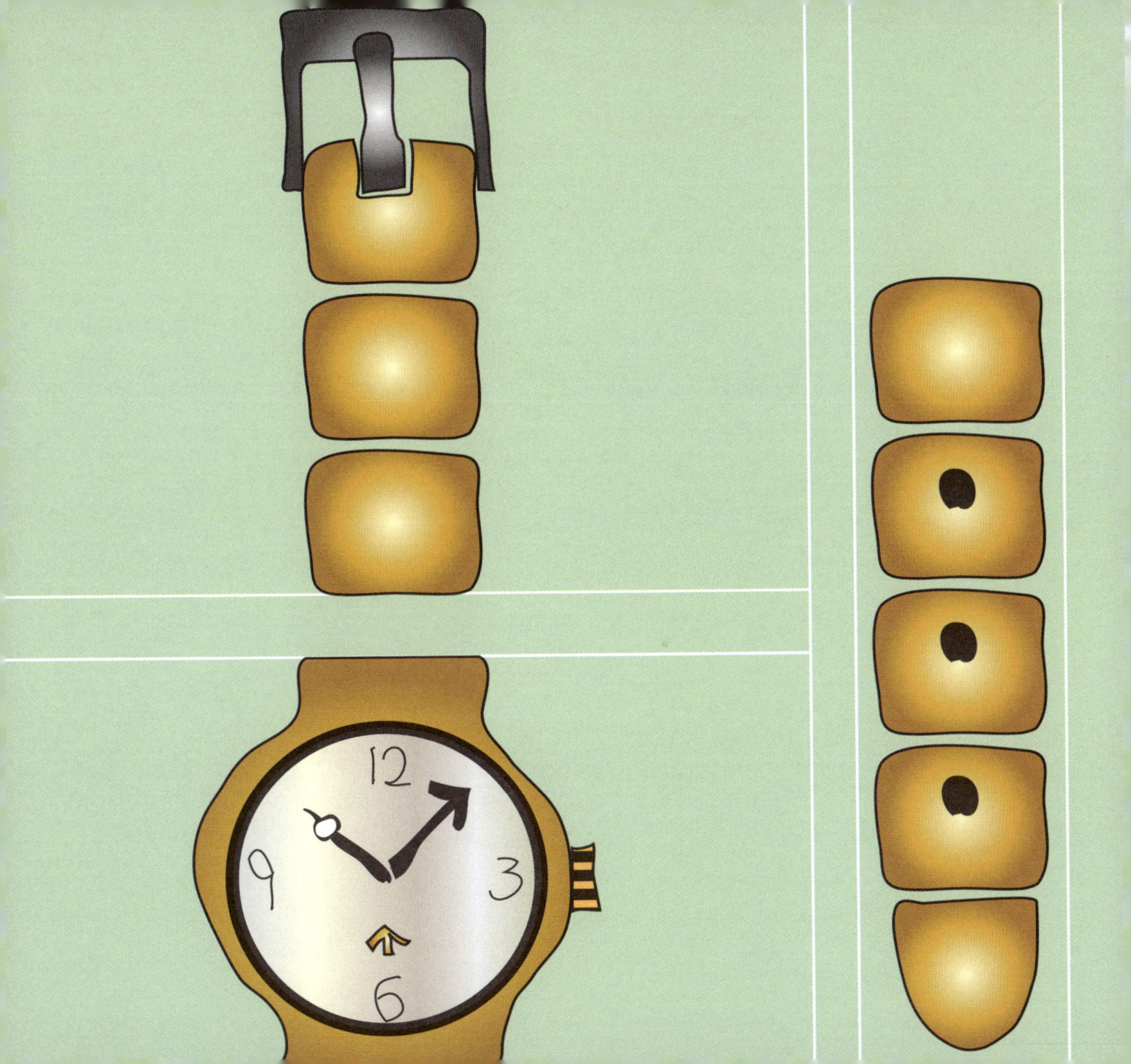
12
3
6
9

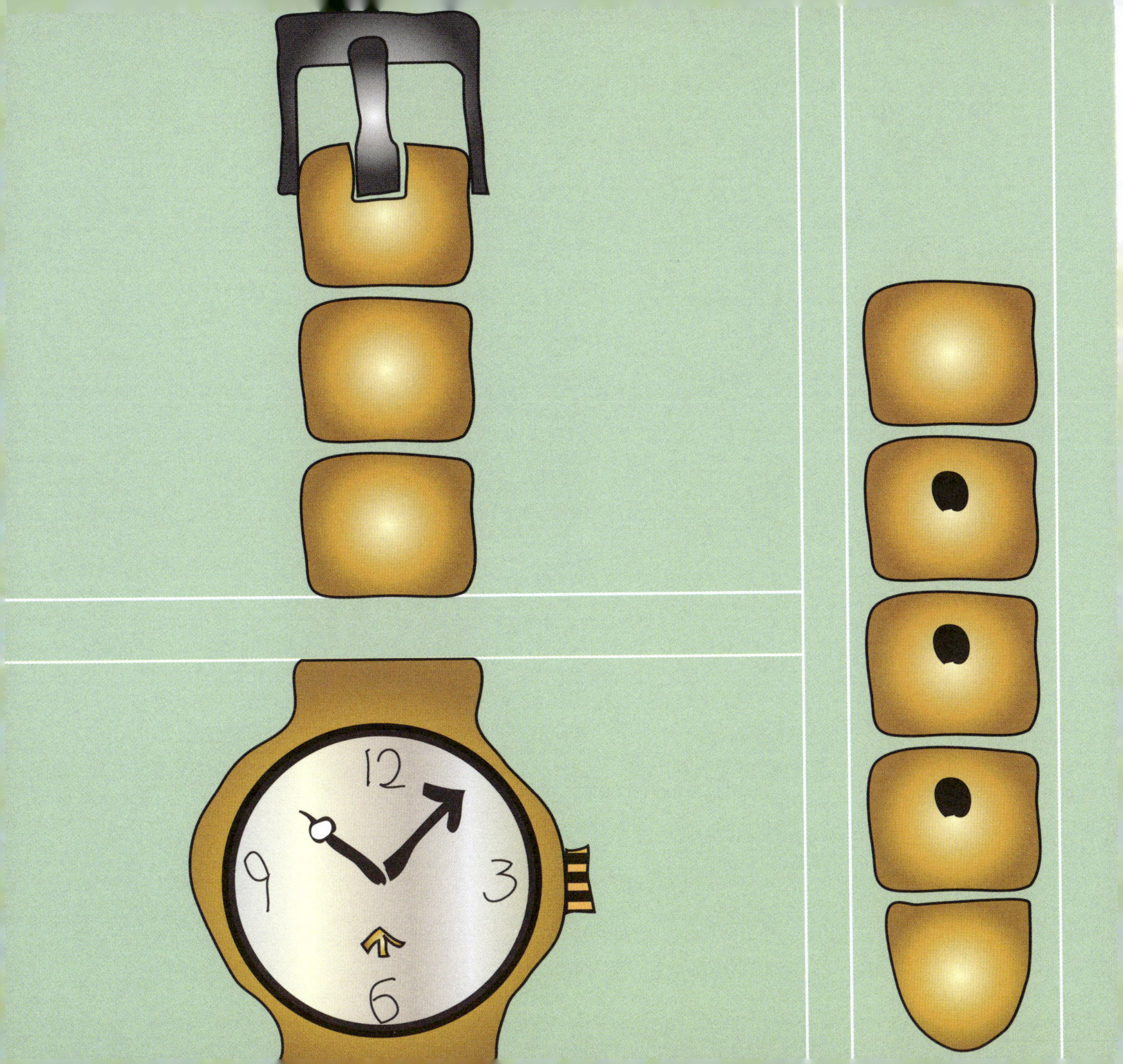
12
3
6
9

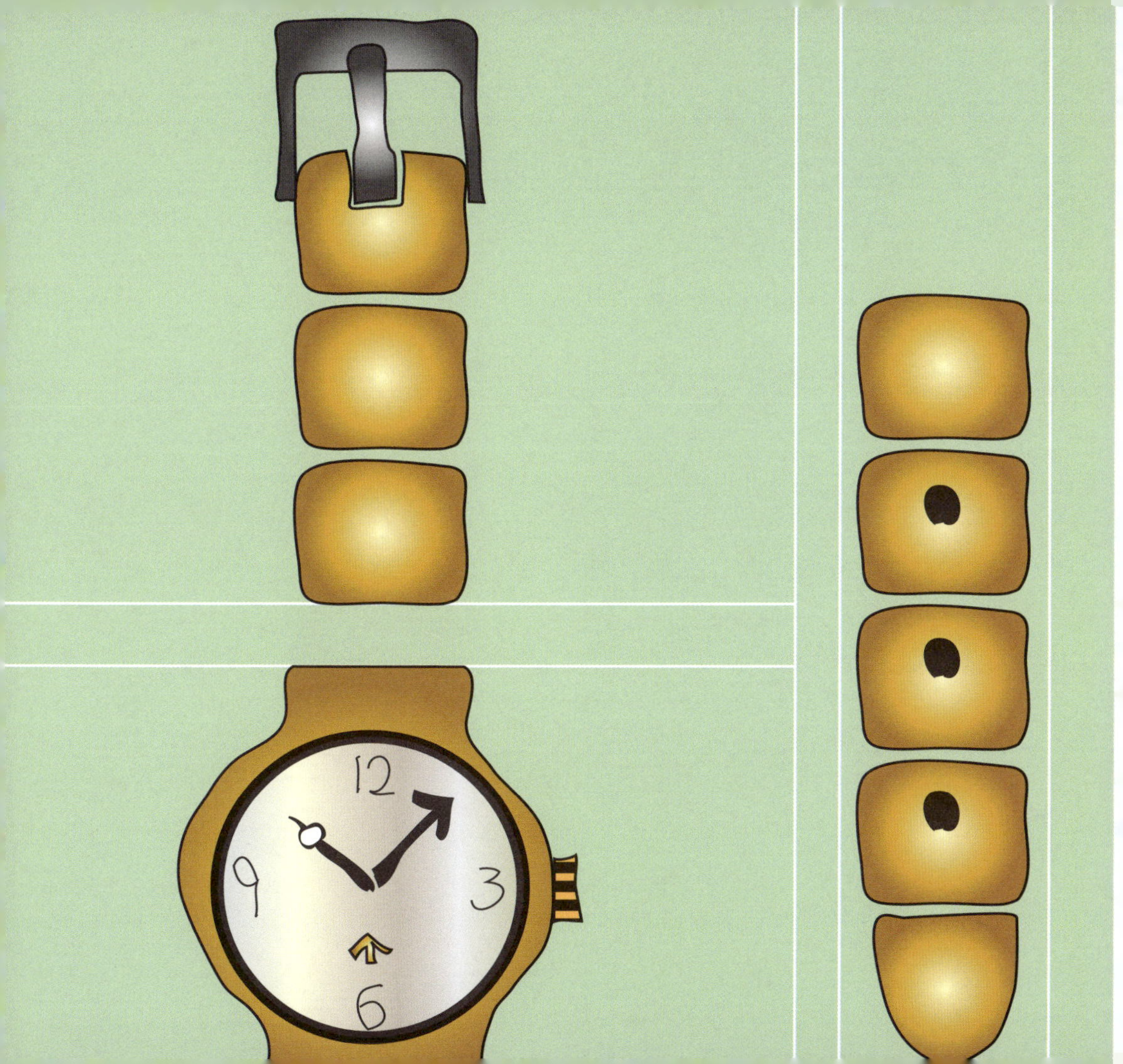
12
3
6
9

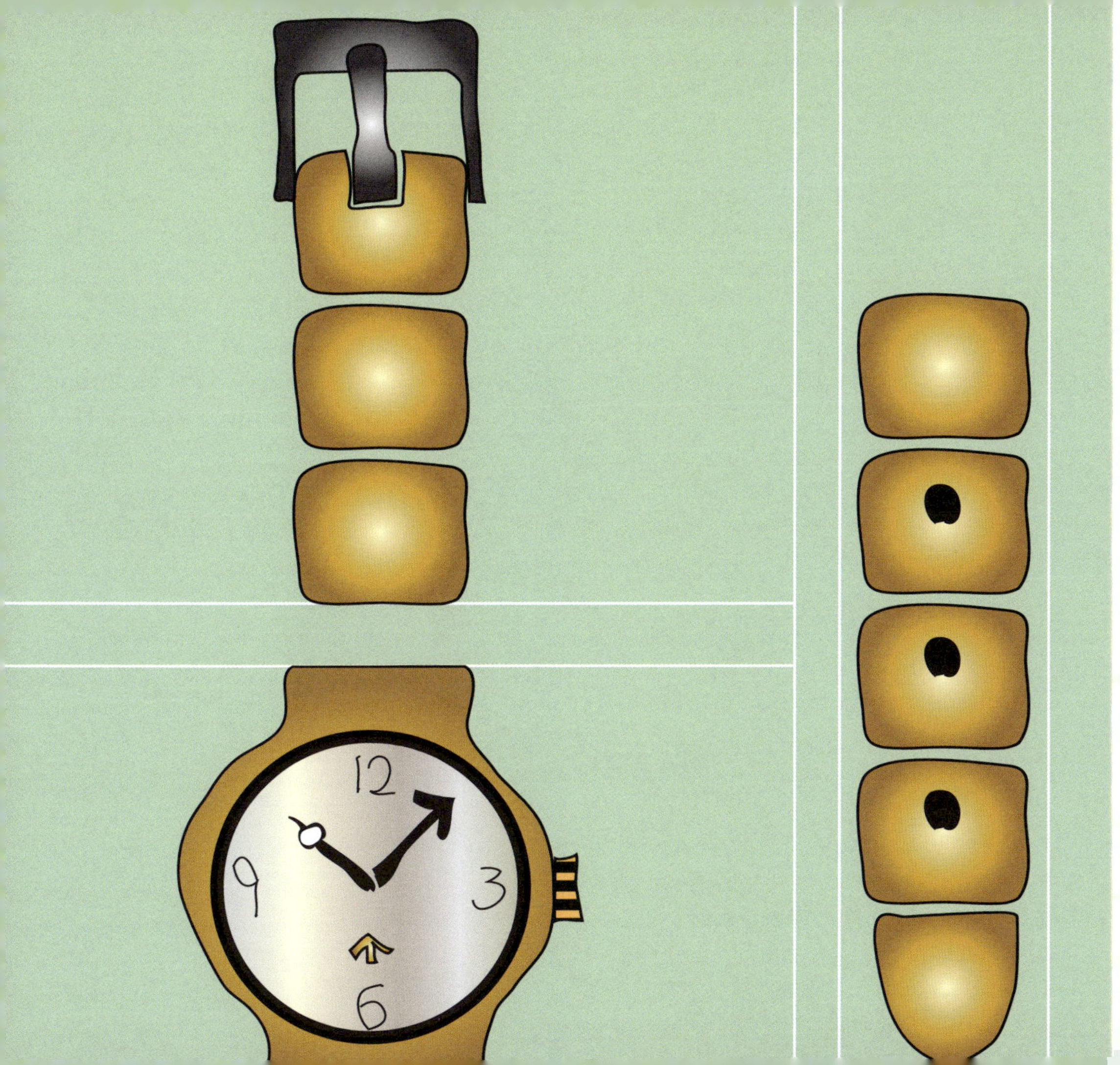
12
9
3
6

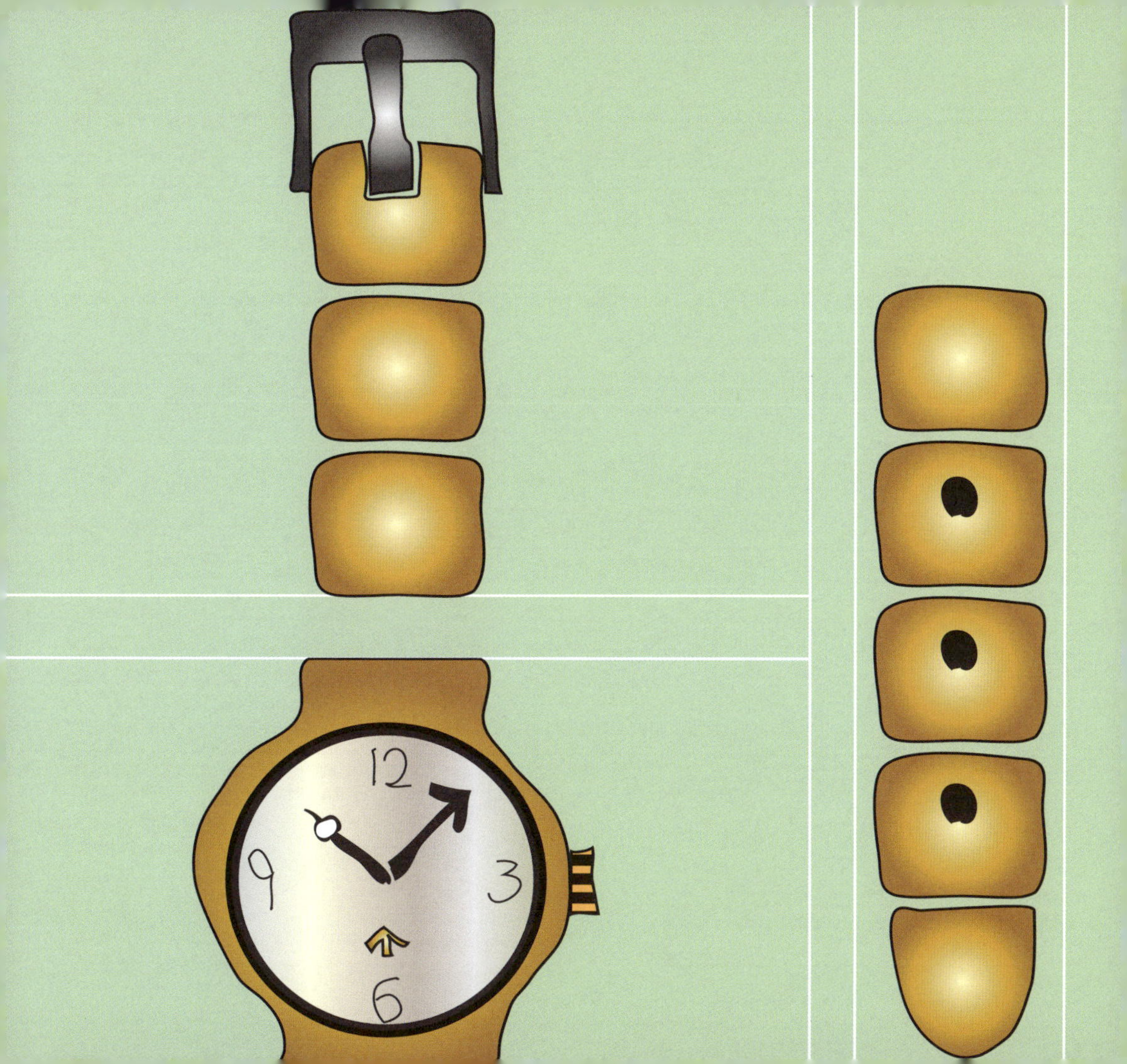

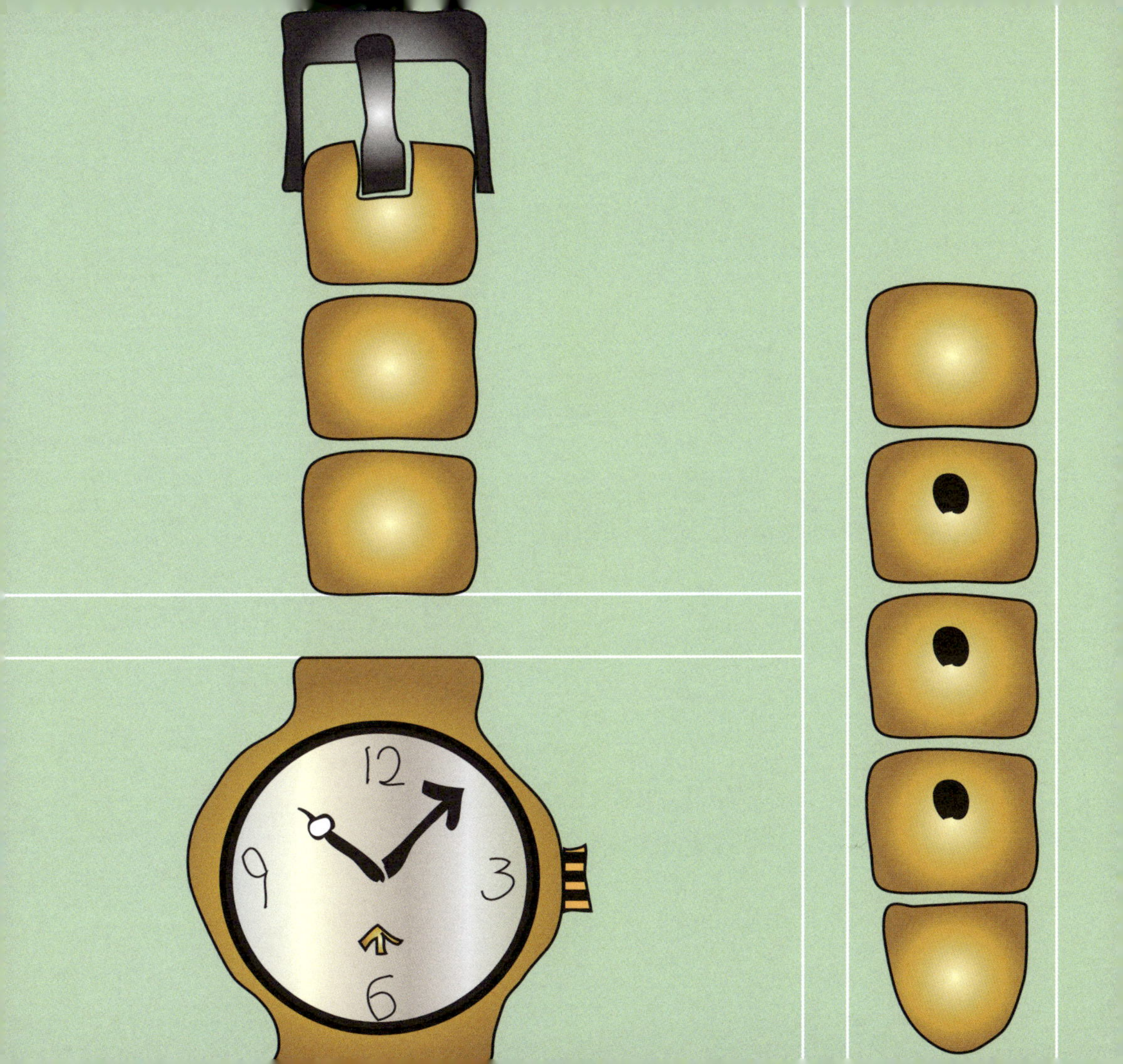
12
9
3
6

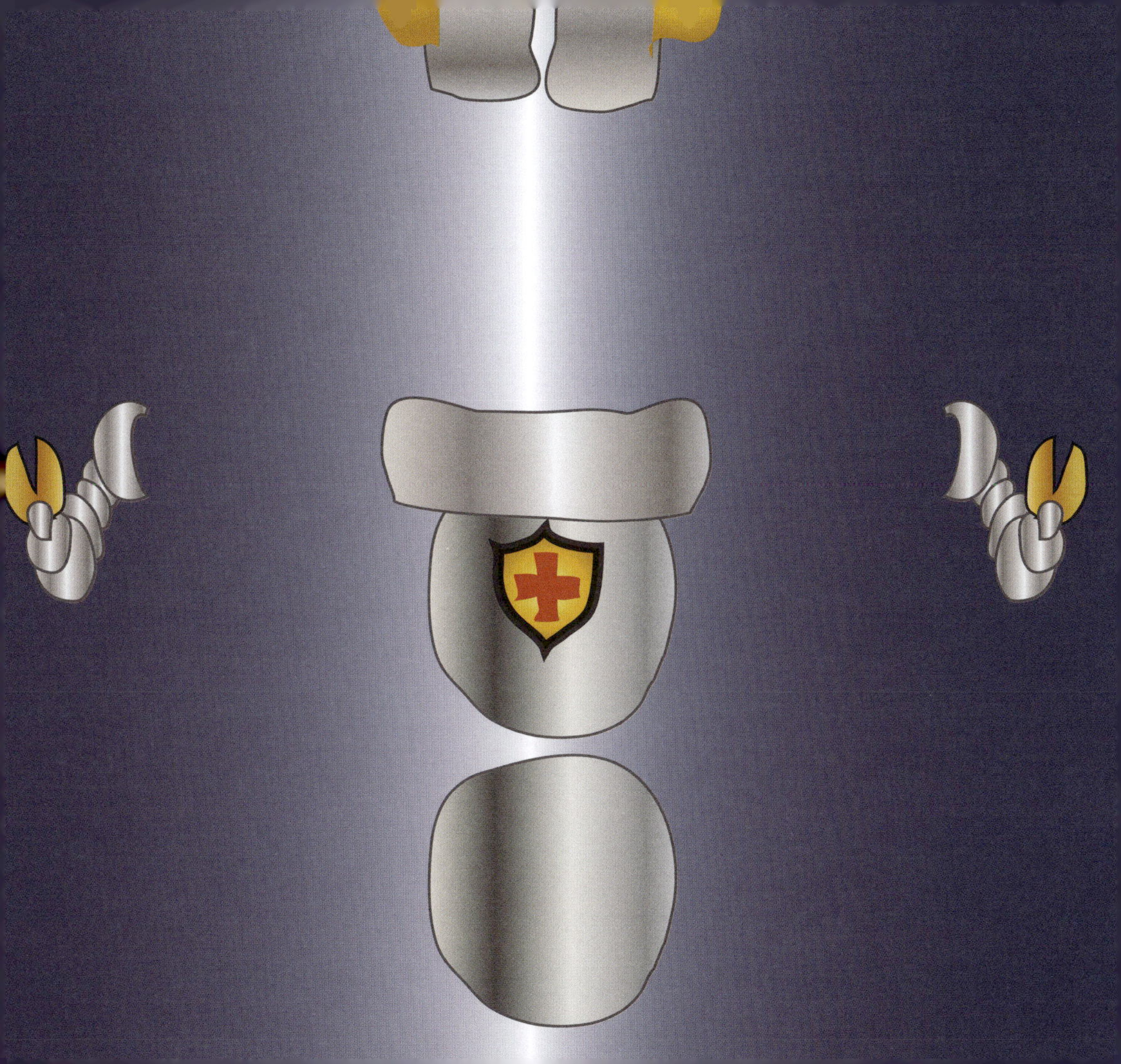

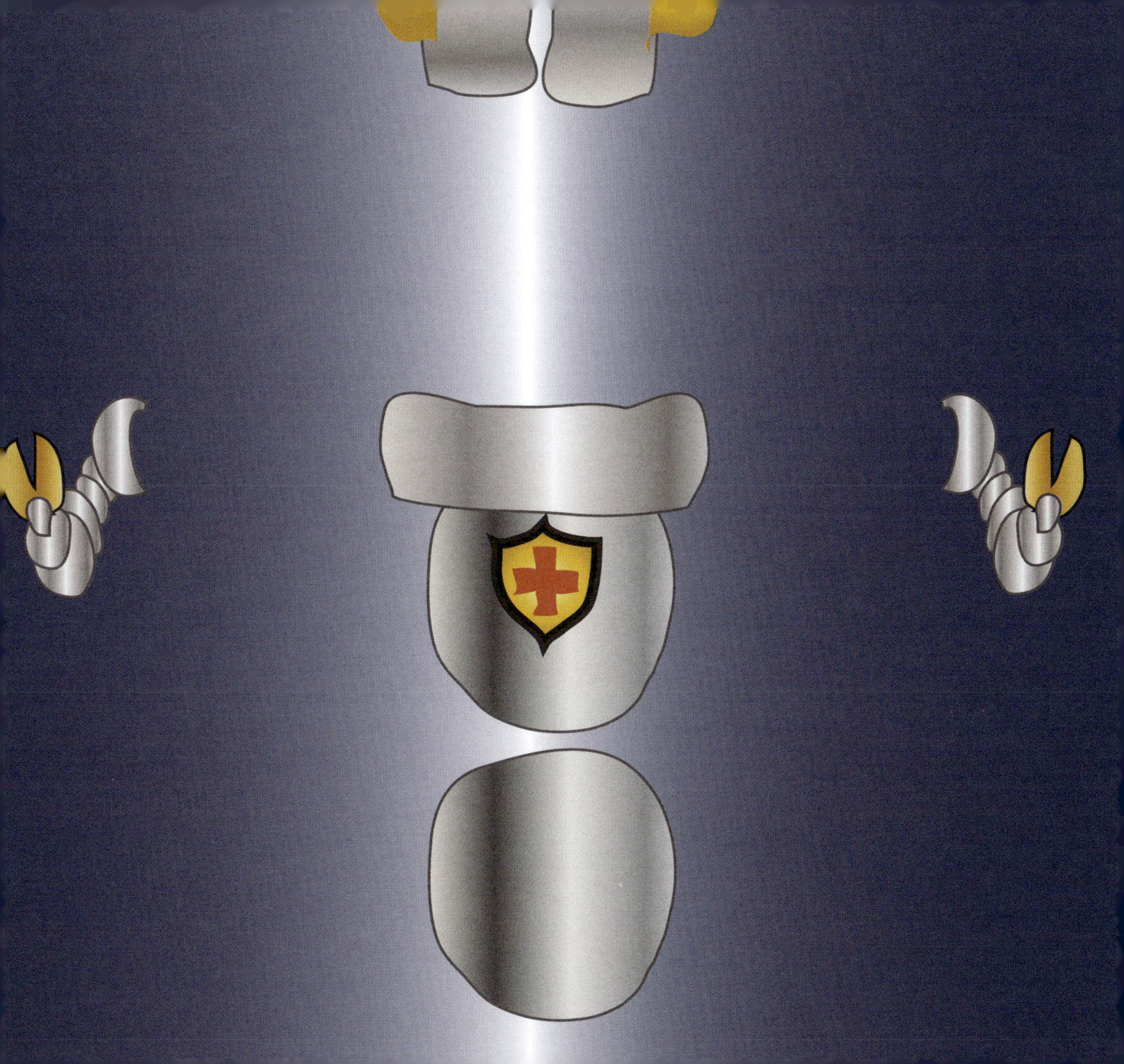

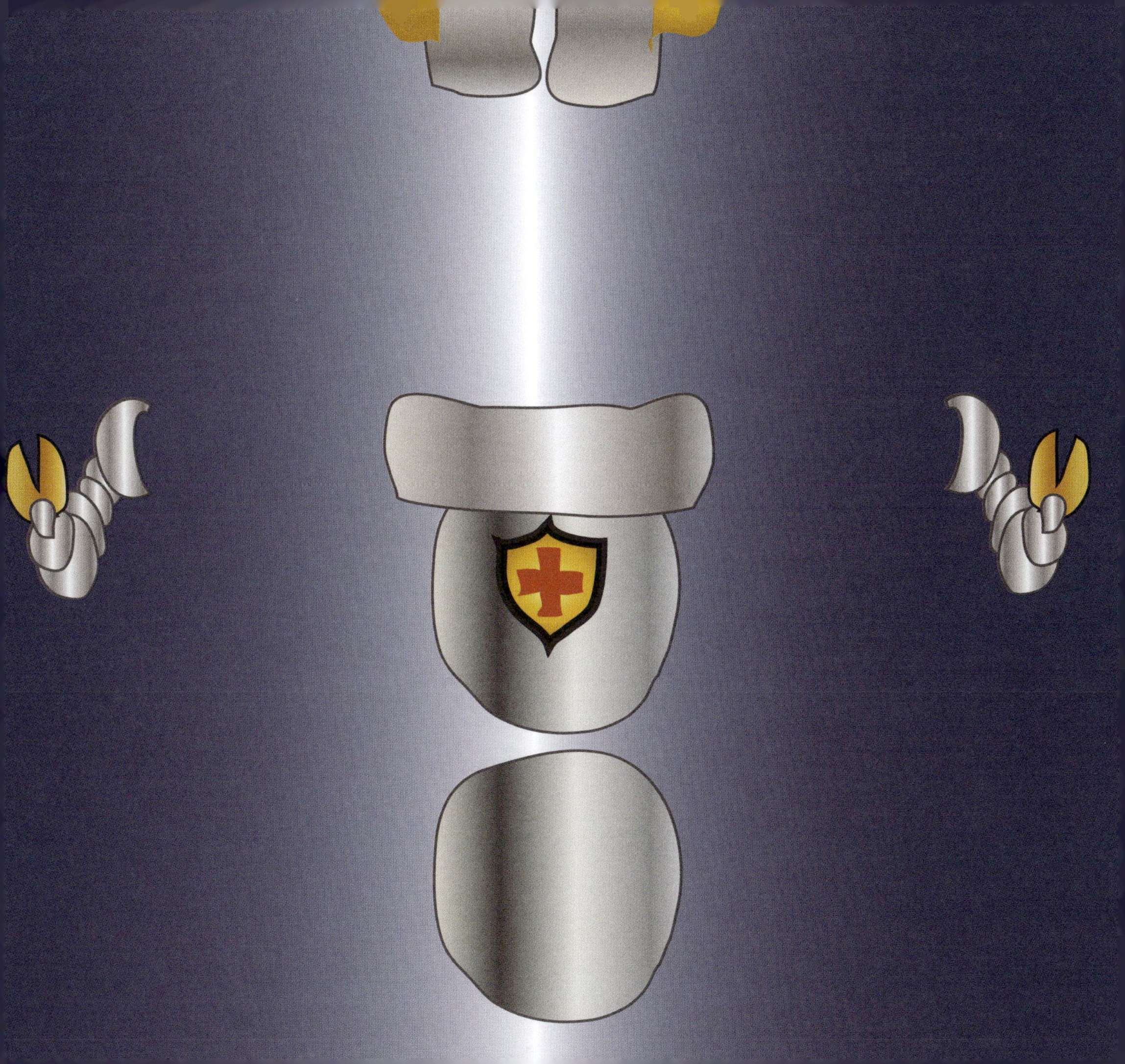

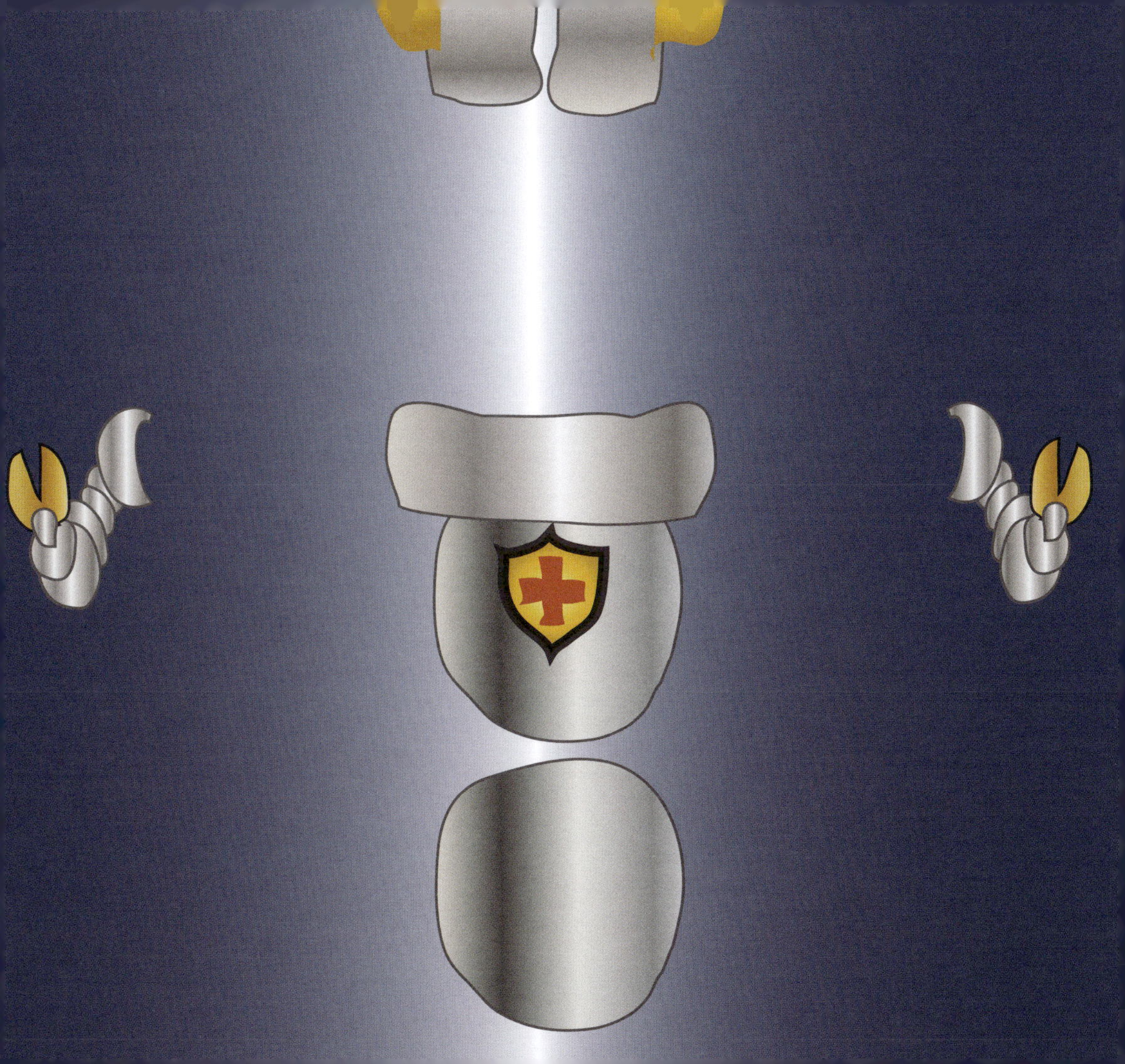

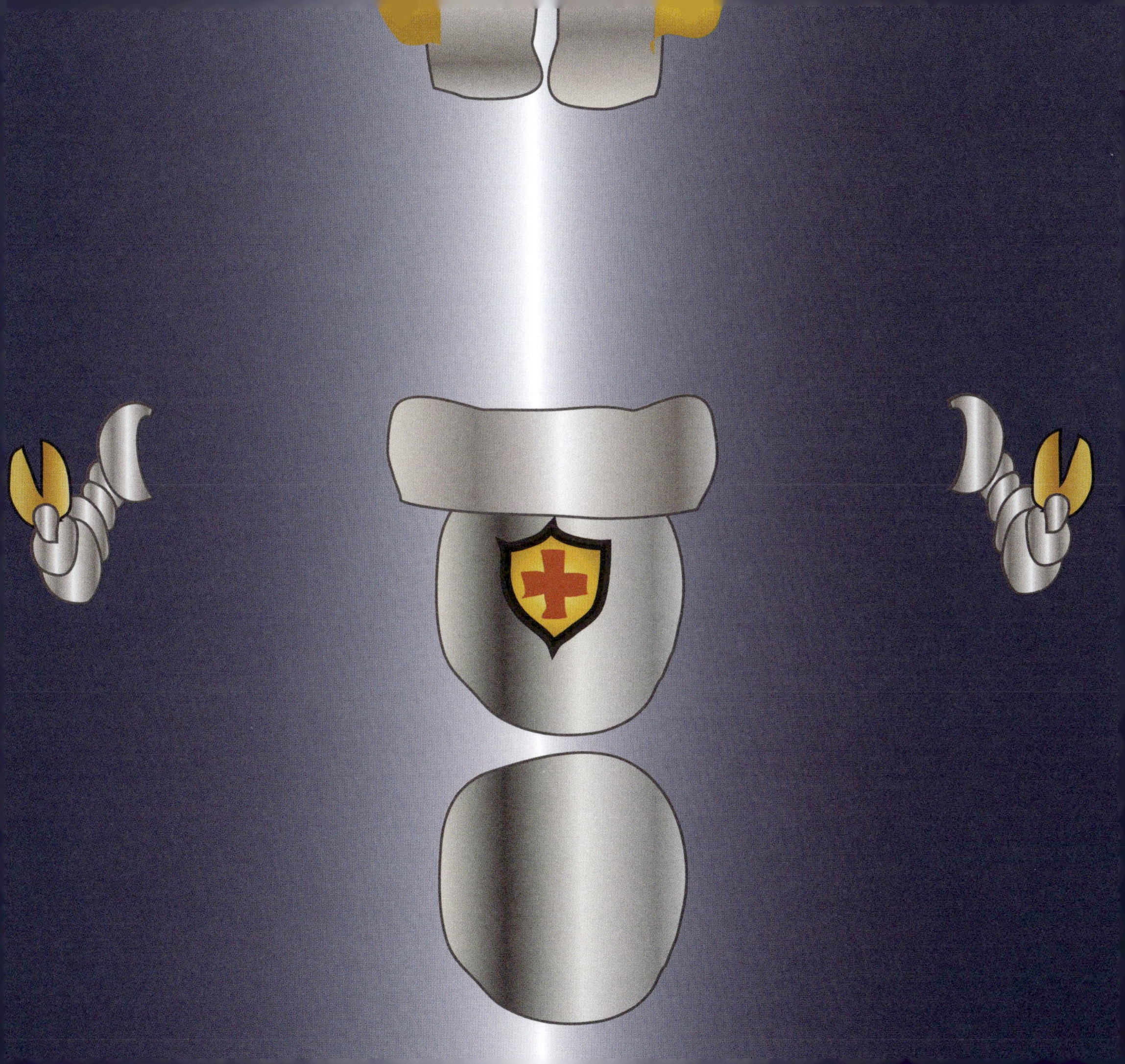

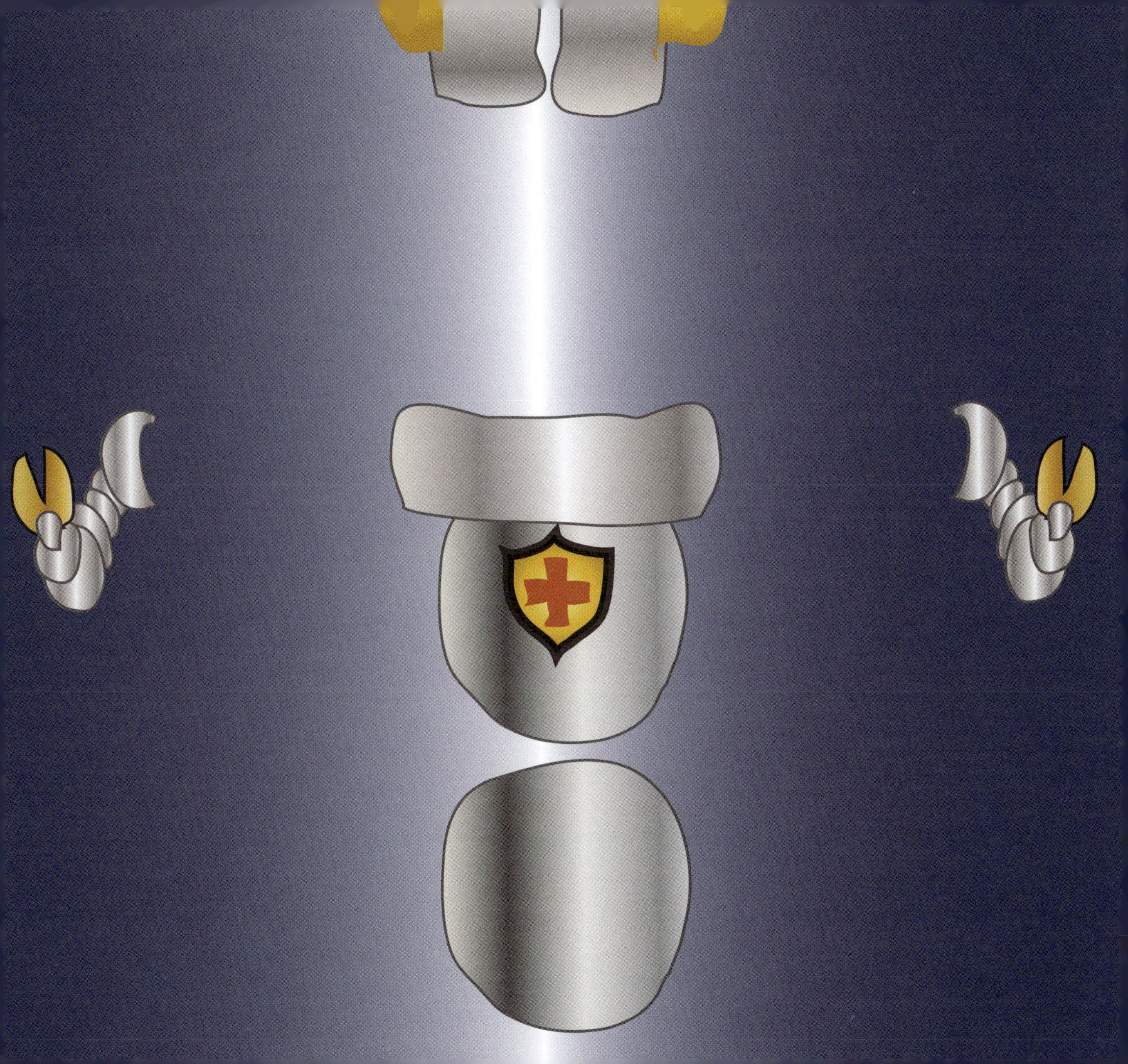

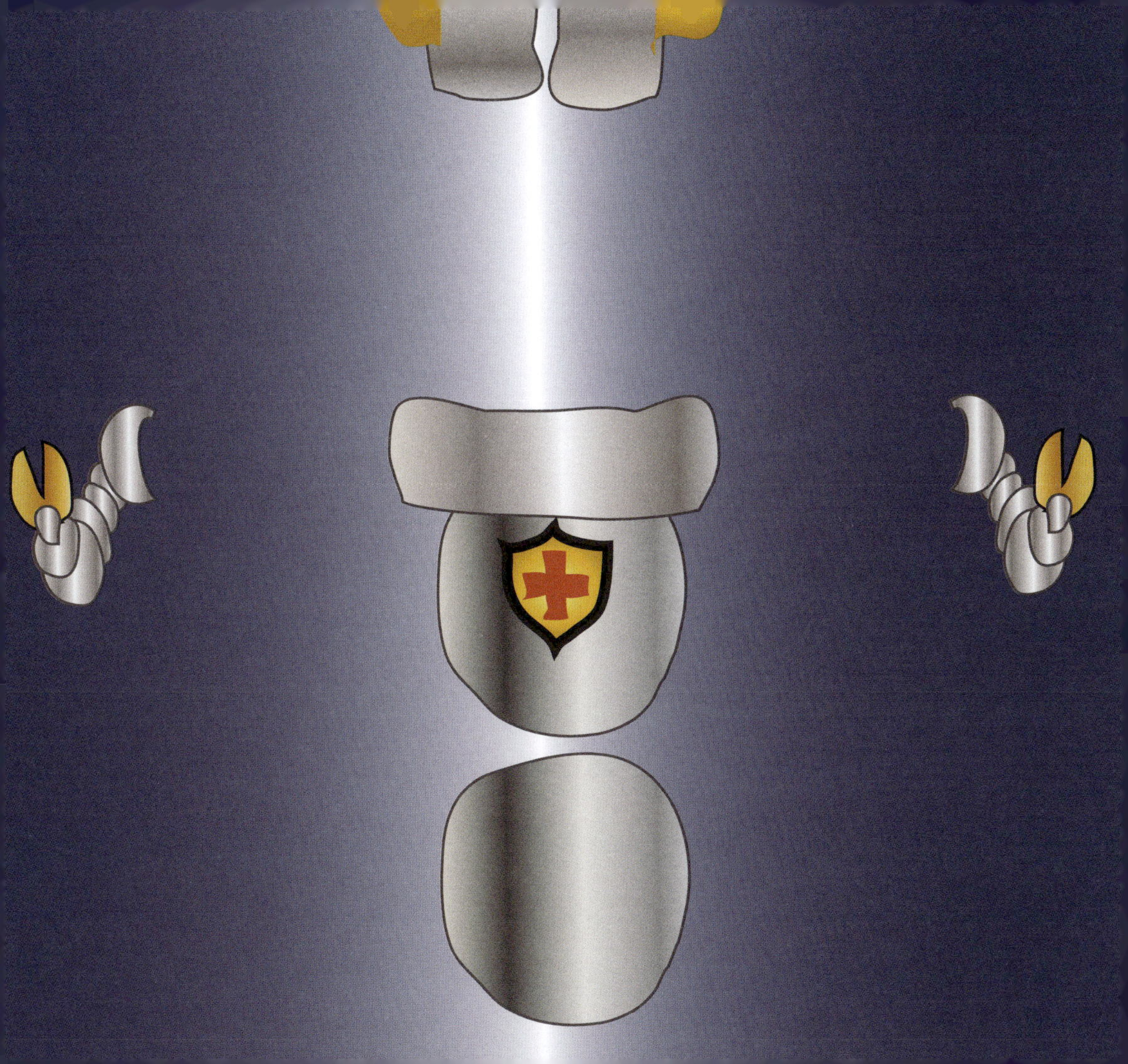

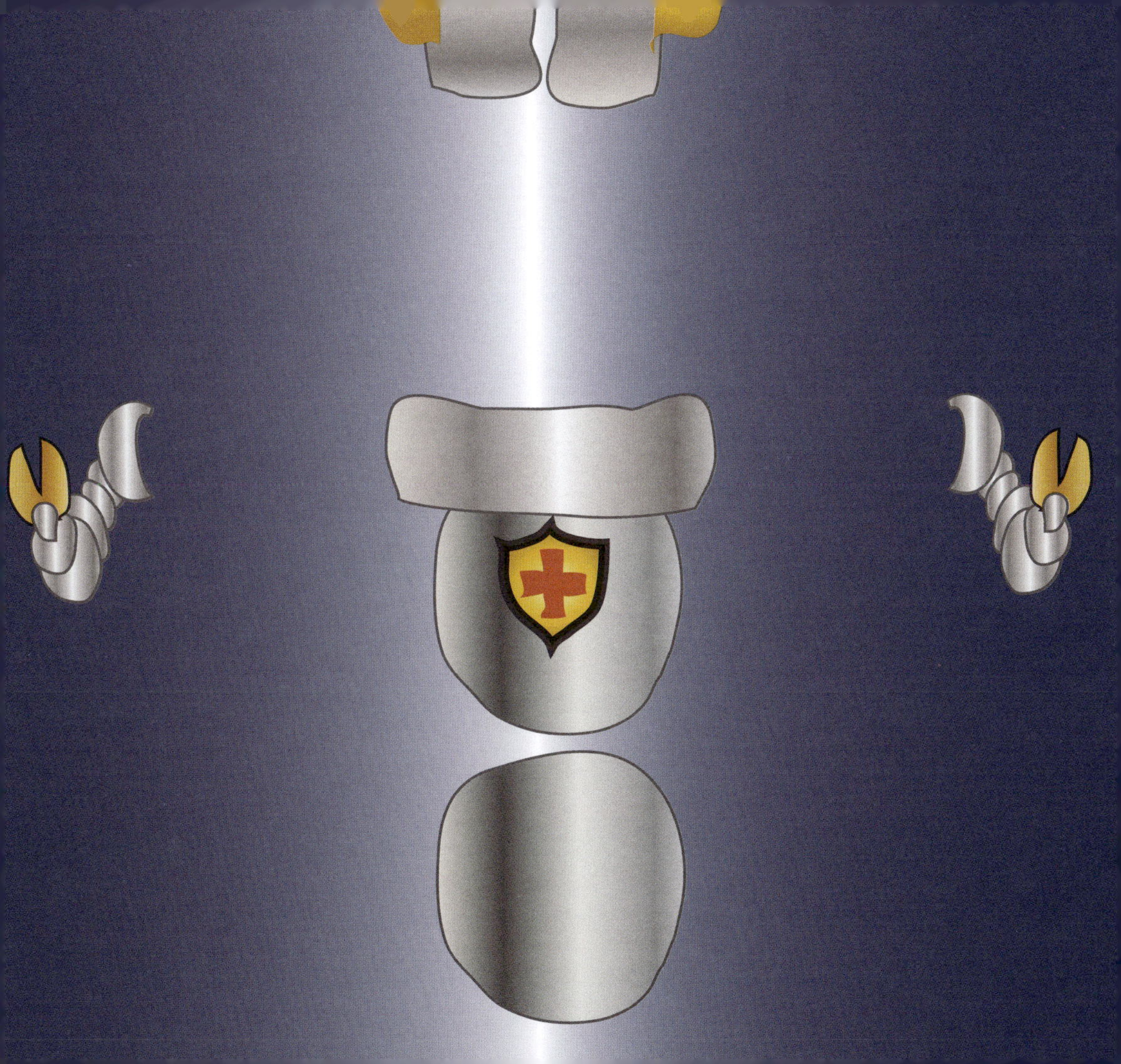

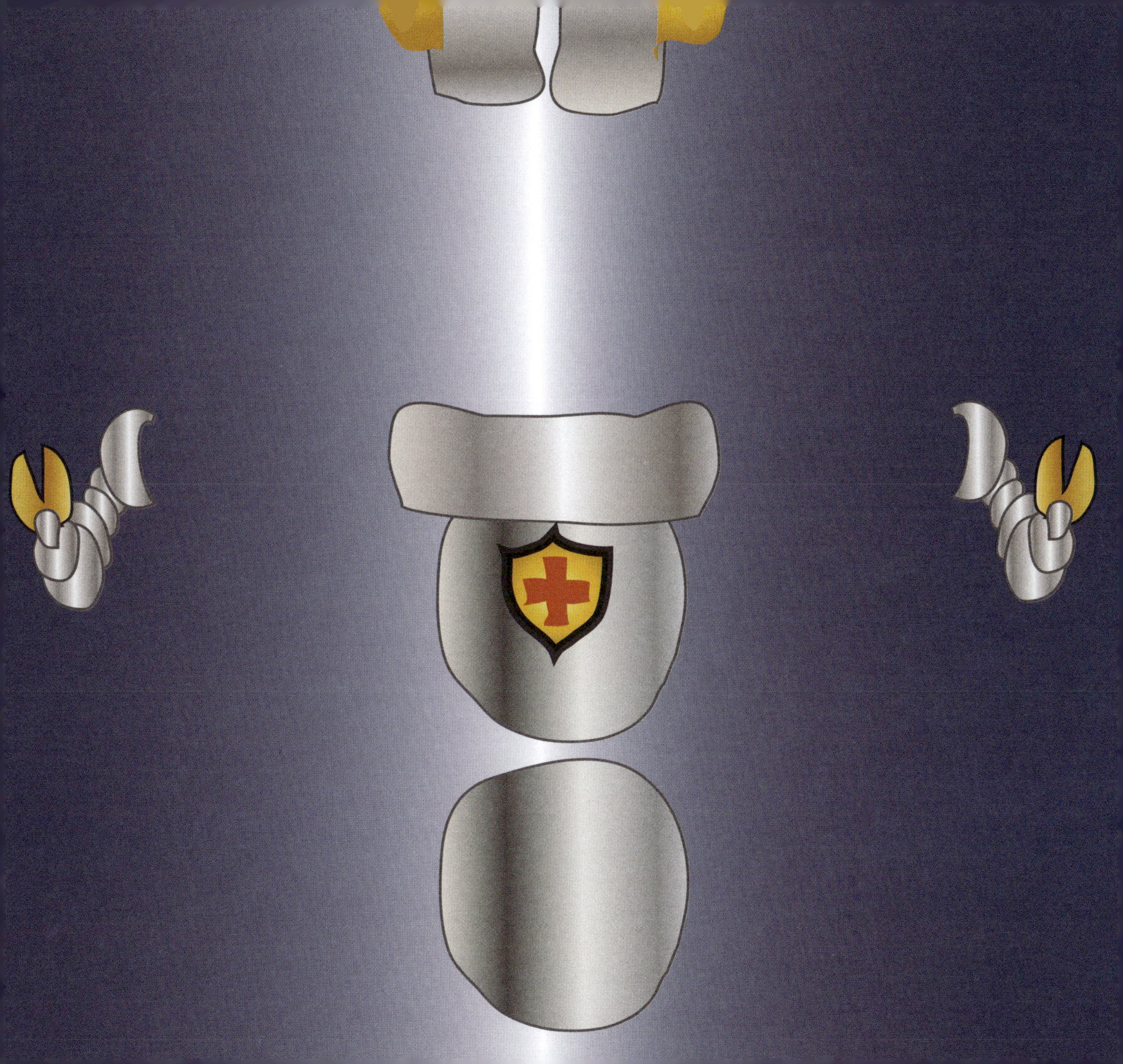

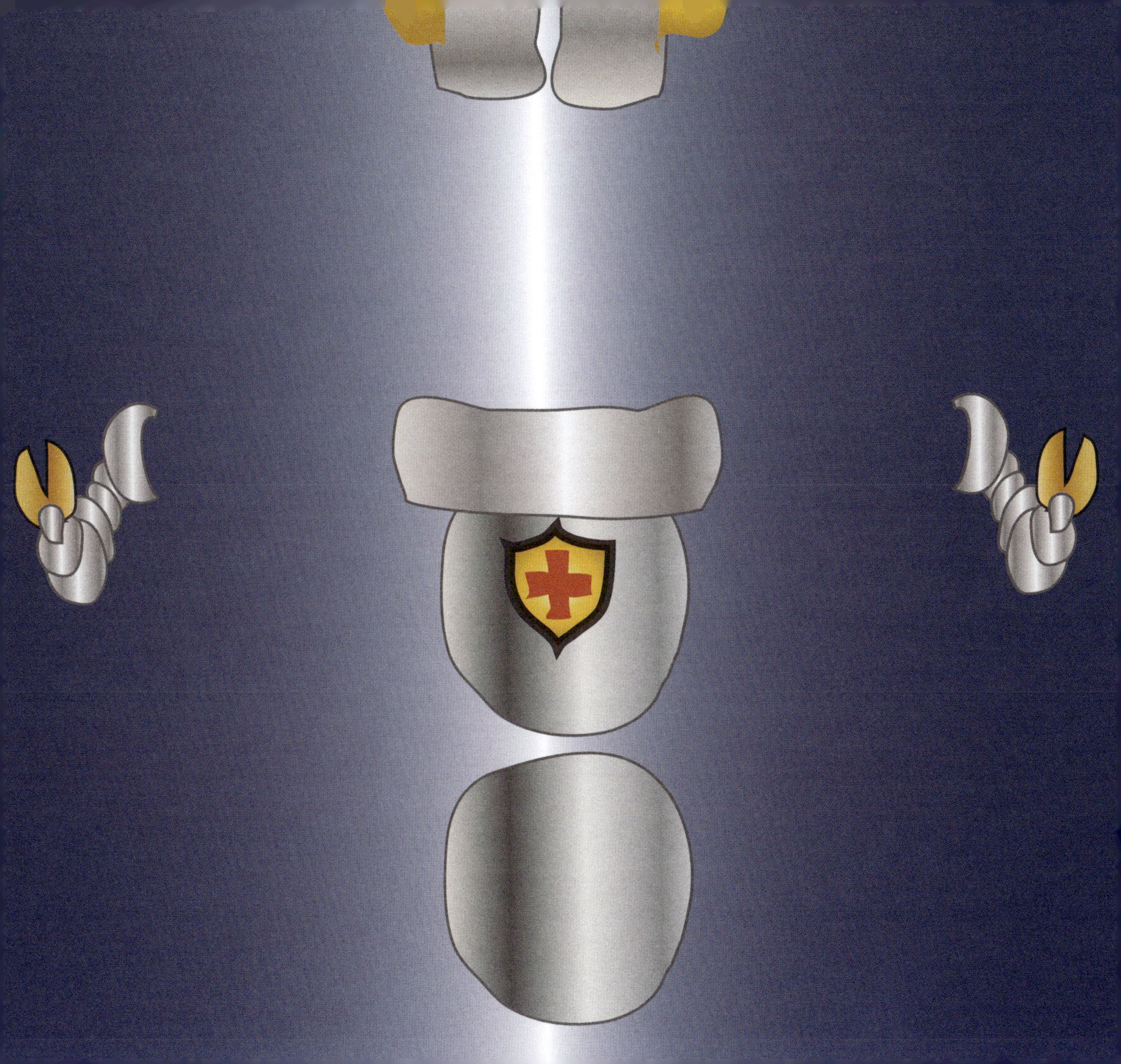

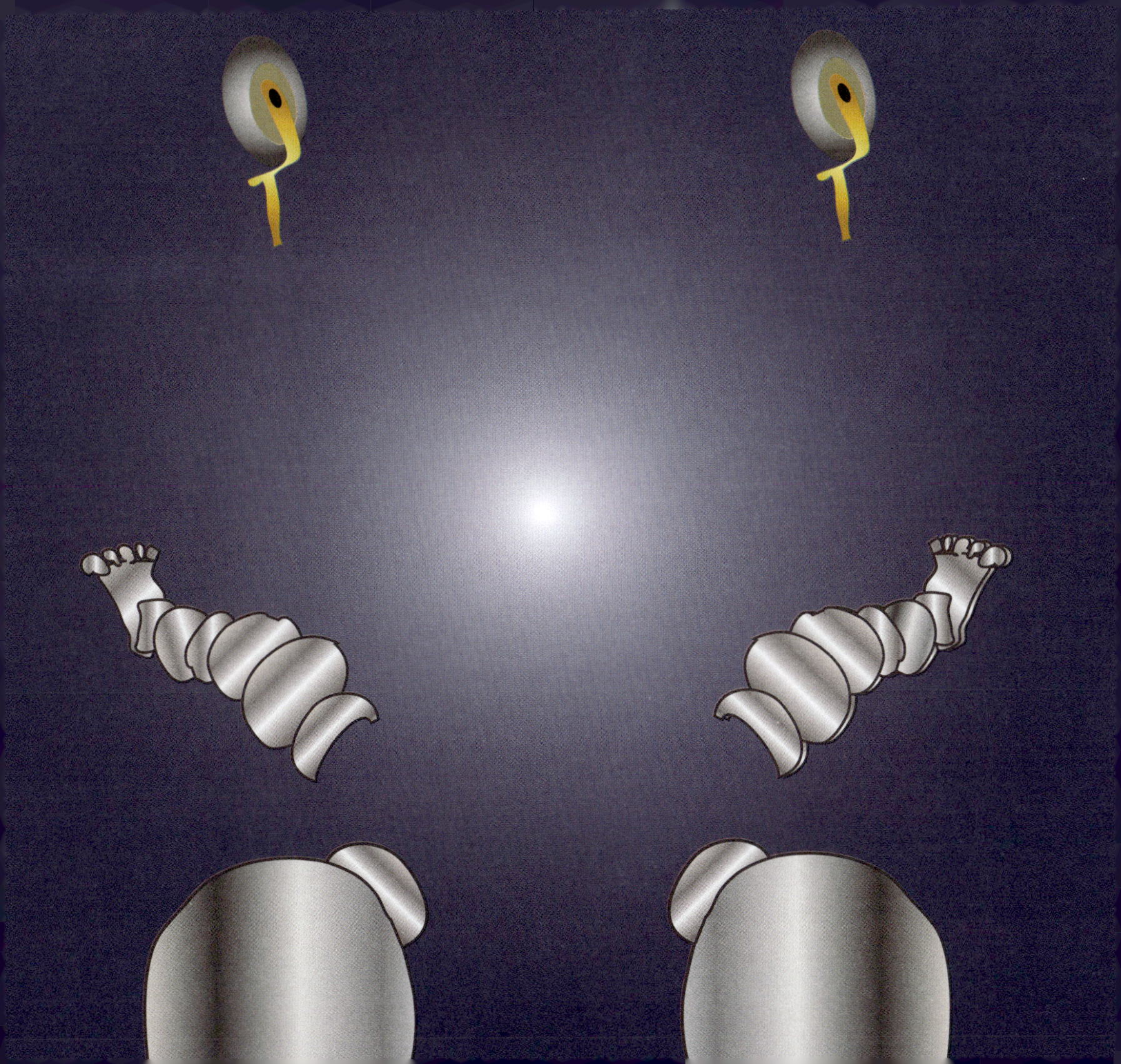

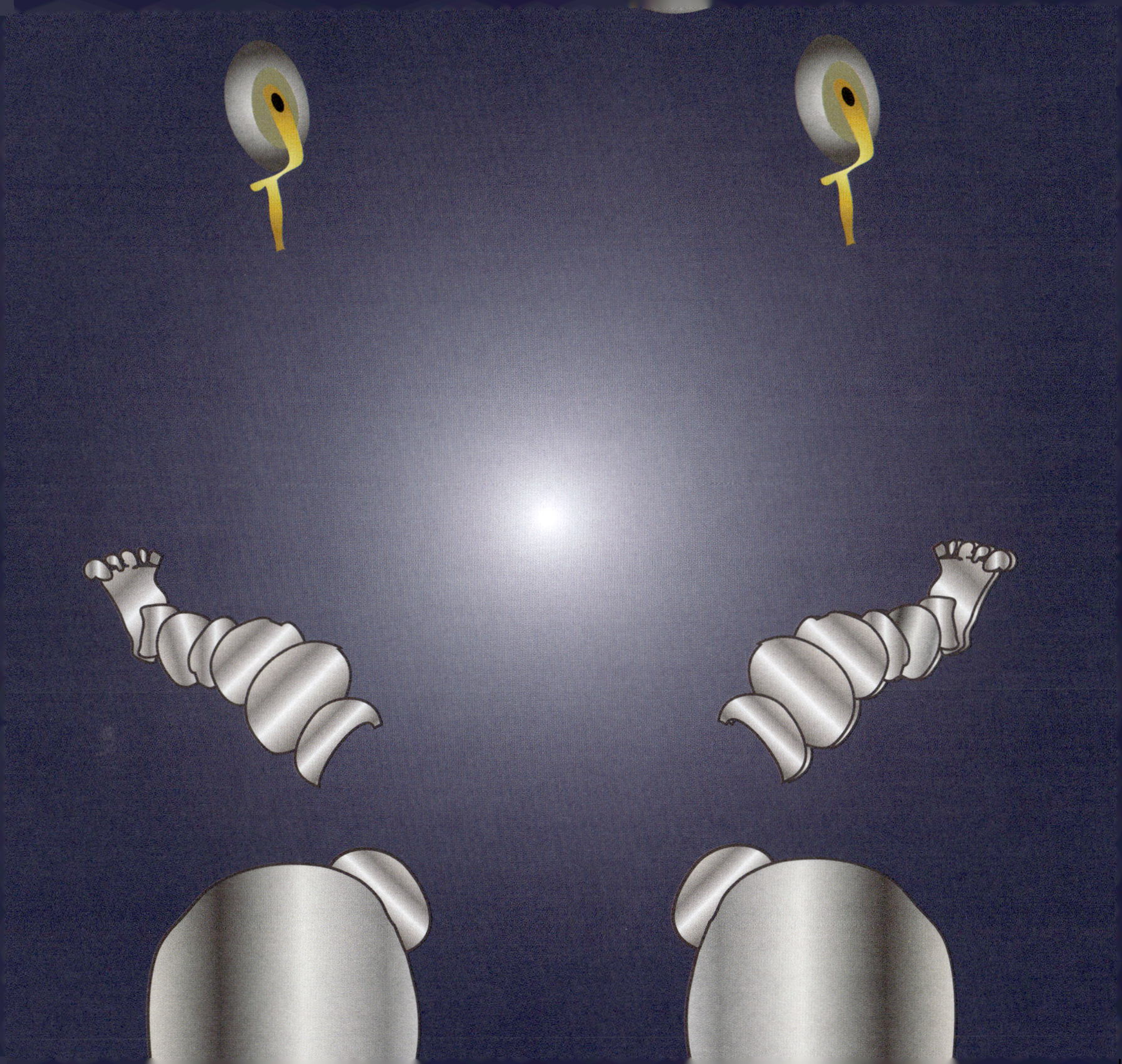

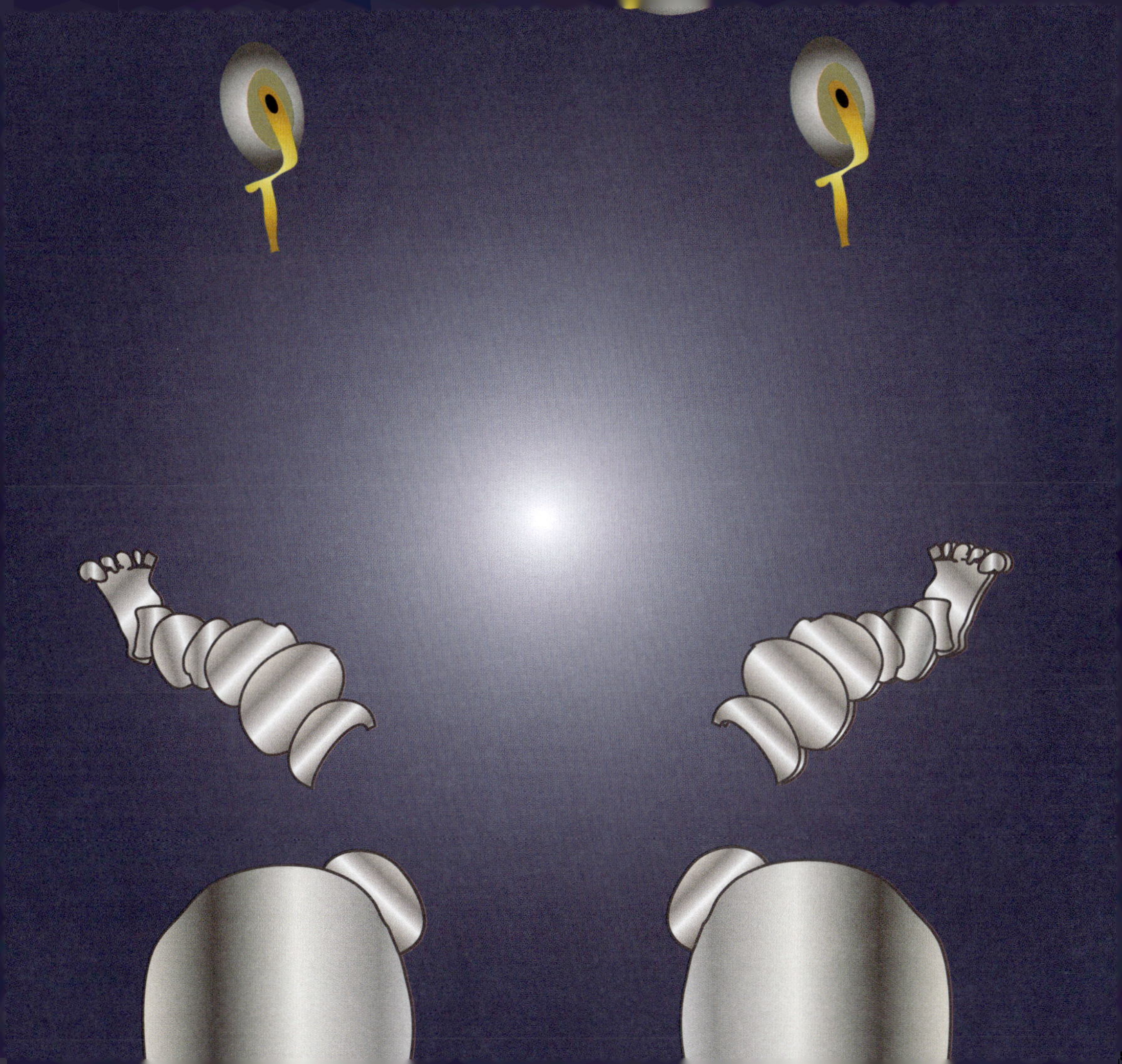

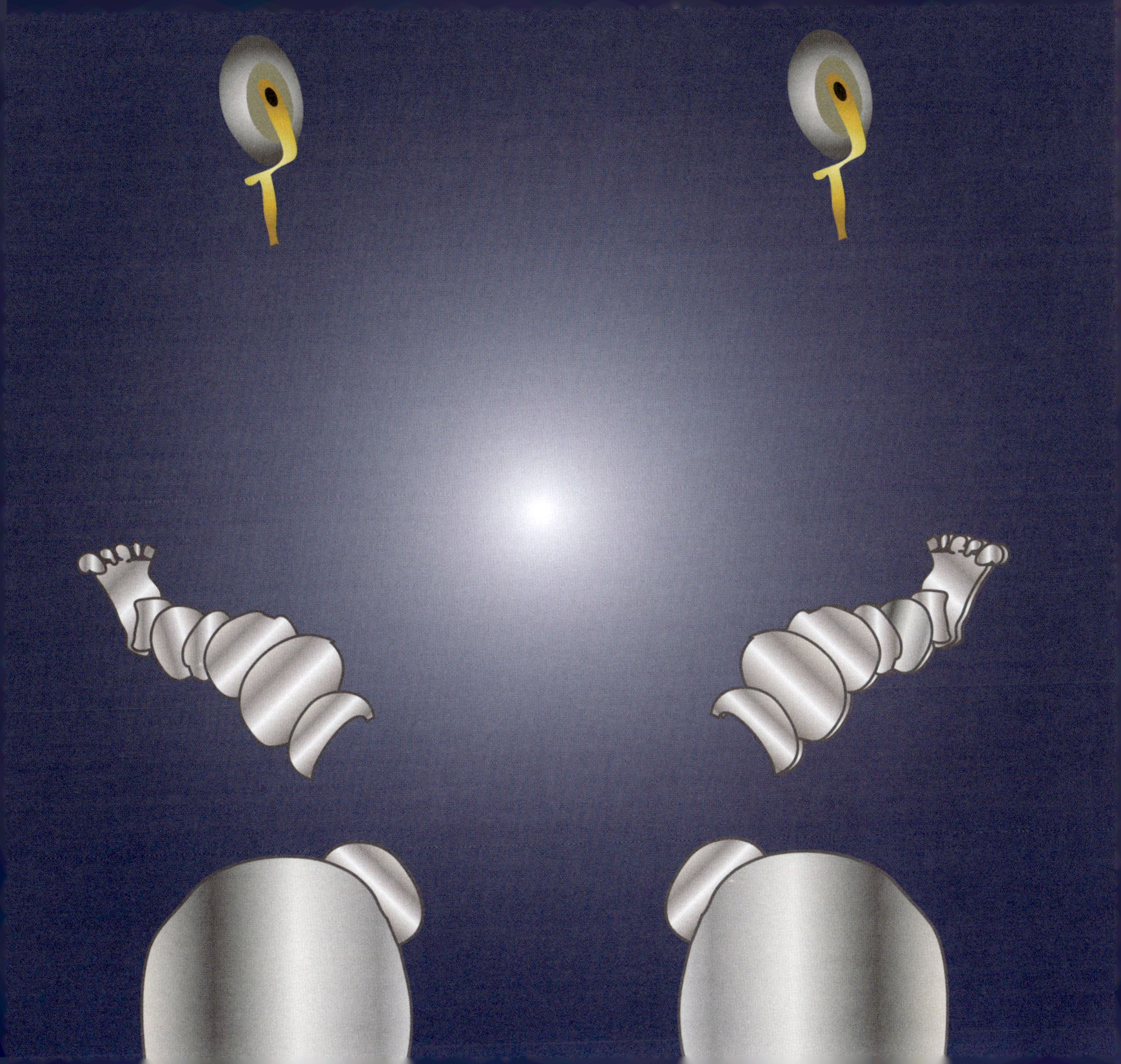

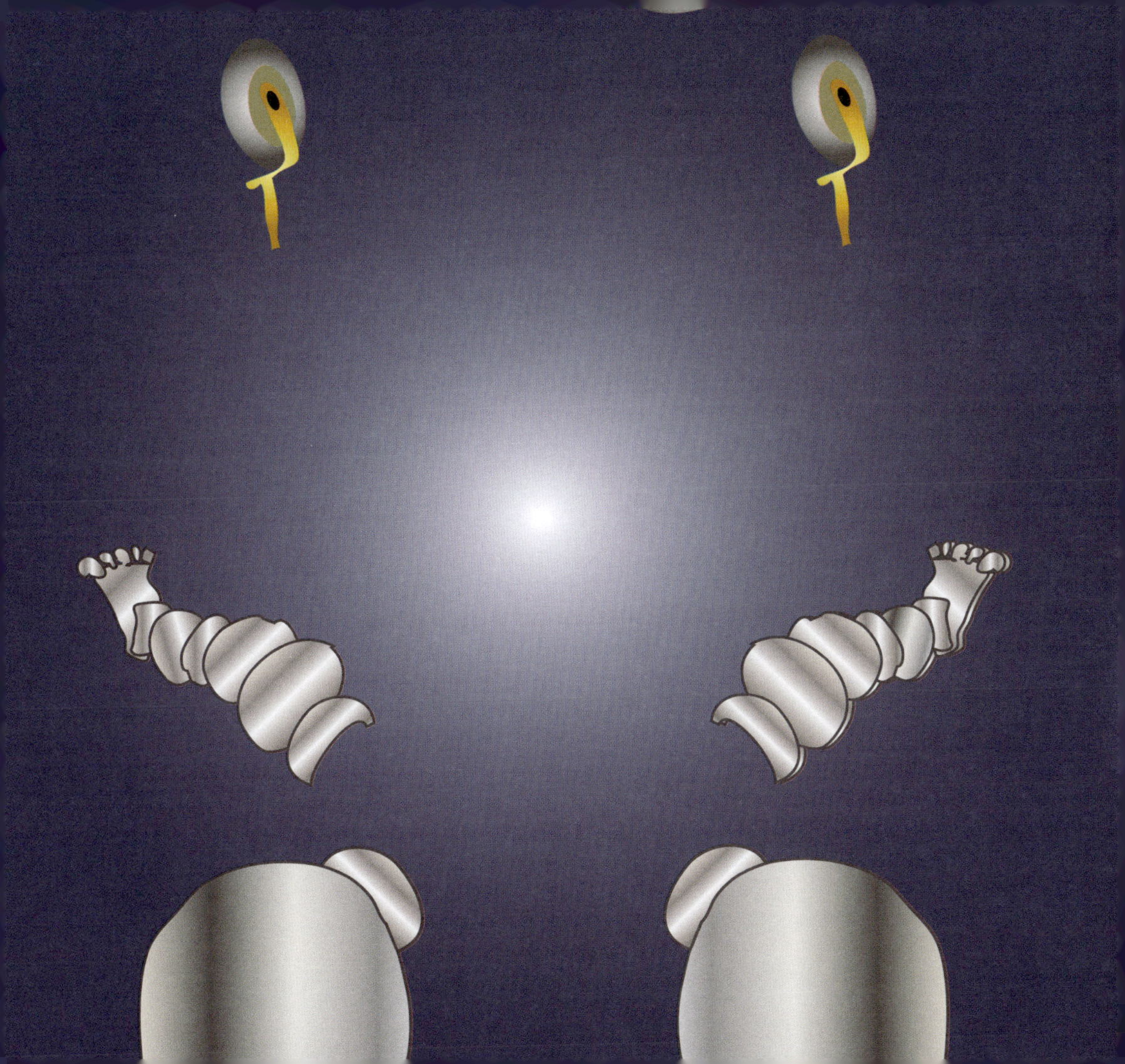

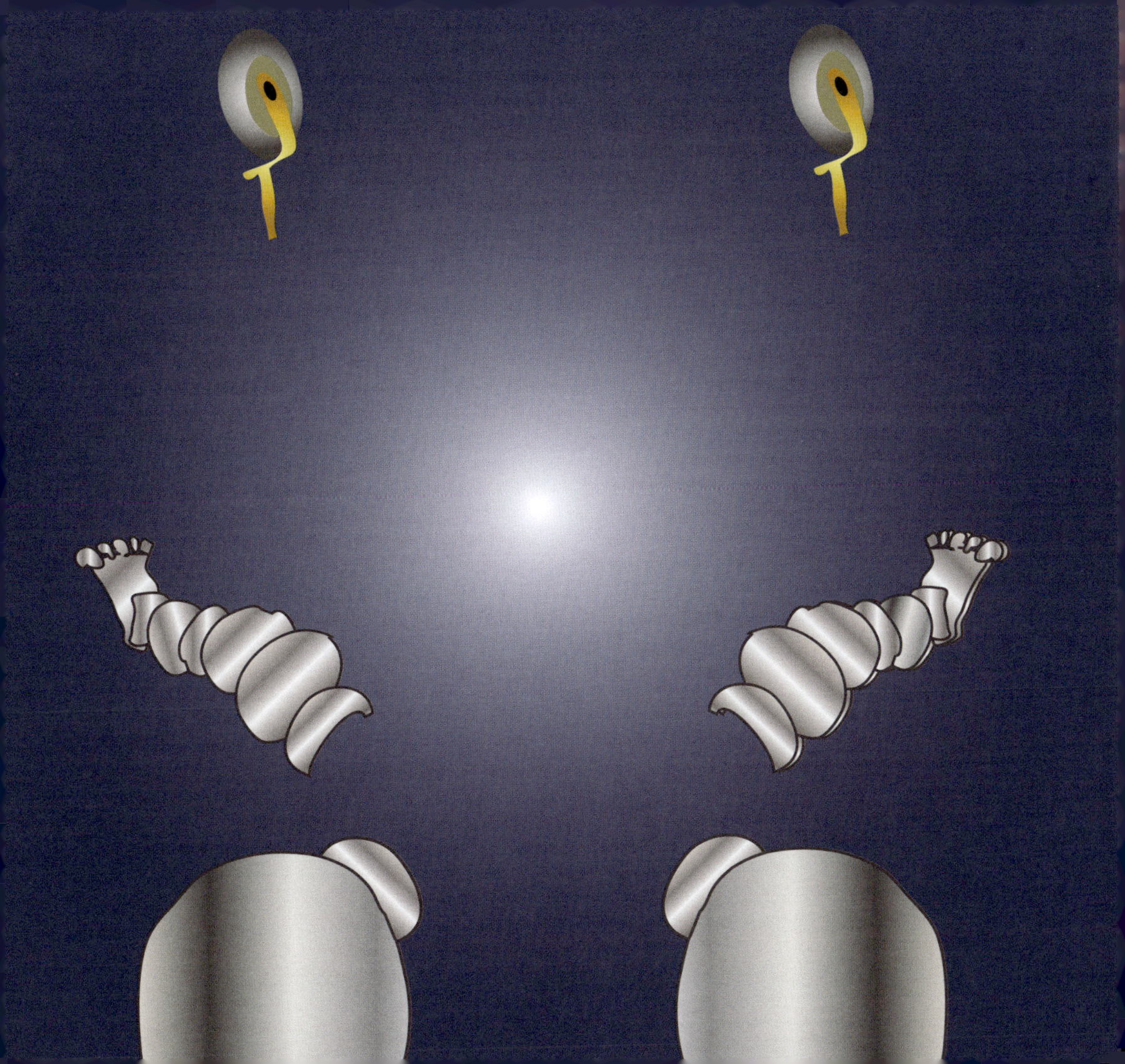

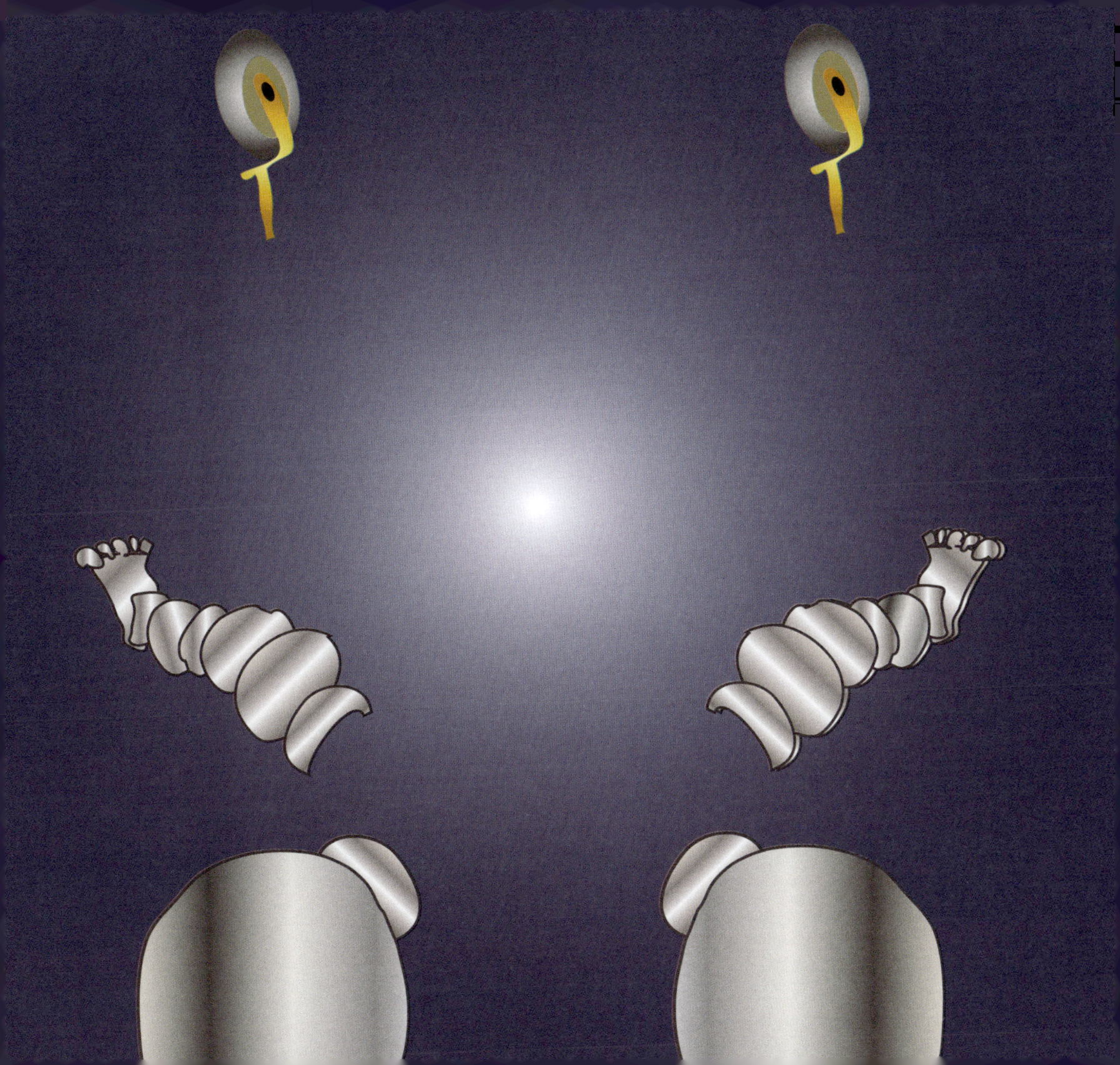

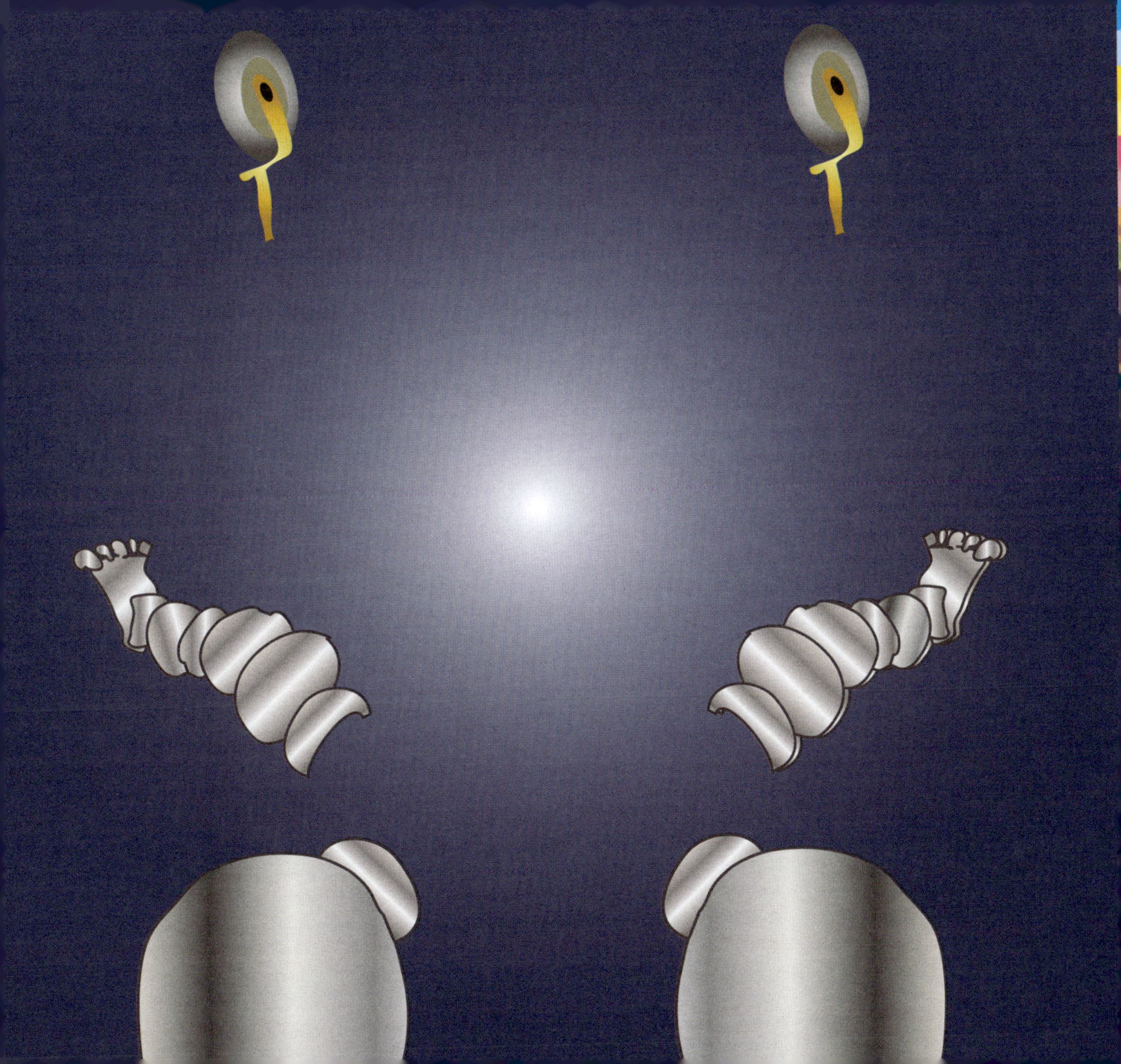

creative Japanese Origami

creative Japanese Origami

15 step-by-step projects to make, plus techniques

mari ono

CICO BOOKS

Published in 2025 by CICO Books
An imprint of Ryland Peters & Small Ltd
20–21 Jockey's Fields
London WC1R 4BW
1452 Davis Bugg Road
Warrenton, NC 27589
www.rylandpeters.com
Email: euregulations@rylandpeters.com

Text and models in this book originally featured in *Origami for Children, Fly Origami Fly,* and *More Origami for Children*

10 9 8 7 6 5 4 3 2 1

A CIP record for this book is available from the British Library.
US Library of Congress CIP data has been applied for.

ISBN: 978-1-80065-427-3

Printed in China

Editor: Robin Gurdon
Photography: Debbie Patterson, Carolyn Barber, Geoff Dann, Terry Benson, and Emma Mitchell
Stylist: Rose Hammick, Rob Merrett, and Trina Dalziel
Contributing project designer: Roshin Ono

Assistant editor: Danielle Rawlings
Senior designer: Emily Breen
Art director: Sally Powell
Creative director: Leslie Harrington
Head of production: Patricia Harrington
Publishing manager: Carmel Edmonds

The authorised representative in the EEA is
Authorised Rep Compliance Ltd.,
Ground Floor. 71 Lower Baggot Street,
Dublin, D01 P593, Ireland
www.arccompliance.com

Safety note: Adults should supervise young children at all times when they are using scissors or glue.

MIX
Paper | Supporting responsible forestry
FSC® C106563
www.fsc.org

CONTENTS

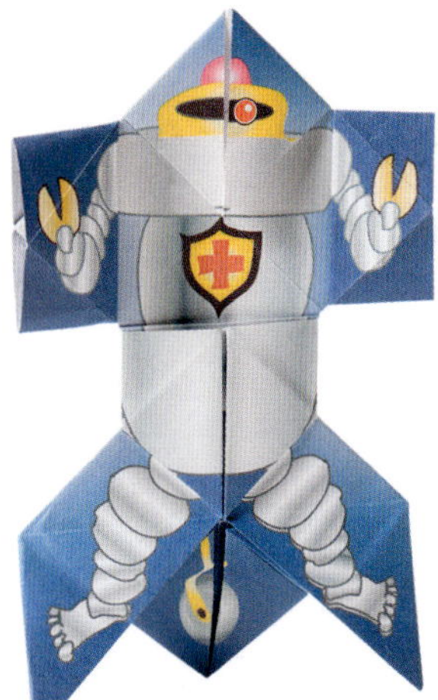

BASIC TECHNIQUES

The most basic skill of origami is folding paper precisely and creating strong, straight creases. This can be achieved through concentration and ensuring folded edges and corners match perfectly before firming up creases. To build up models, more complicated folds are needed to ensure the paper retains its shape.

MAKING FOLDS

Making the paper fold as crisply and evenly as possible is the key to making models that will look as the designs intend–it really is as simple as that.

1 When you make a fold ensure that the paper lies exactly where you want it, with the corners sitting exactly on top of each other.

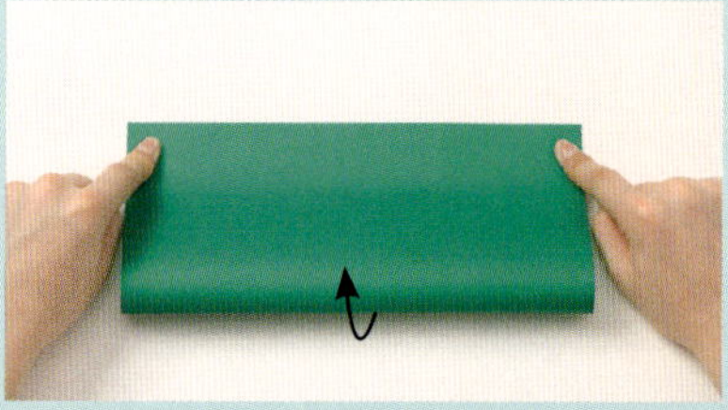

2 As you make the crease be sure to keep the paper completely still so that the fold is perfectly true and straight.

3 Still holding the paper with your spare hand use a ruler or perhaps the side of a pencil to press down the fold until it is as flat as possible.

OPENING FOLDS

Sometimes you will need to open out a crease and refold the paper so that it lies in a new shape, as in the triangle fold shown here.

1 Lift the flap to be opened out and begin pulling the two sides apart.

2 As the space widens you will need to be sure that the far point folds true, so use a pencil to gently prise the paper open.

3 As the two corners separate the top point drops forward and the two edges open out to become one.

4 Press down the new creases to make the two new angled sides of the triangle.

KEY TO ARROWS

FOLDING DIRECTION

Fold the entire paper over in the direction of the arrow.

MAKE A CREASE

Fold the paper in the direction of the arrow, then unfold again to make a crease.

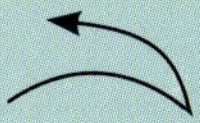

OPEN OUT

Open out and refold the paper in the direction shown.

TURN OVER

Turn the paper over without changing the top and bottom edges.

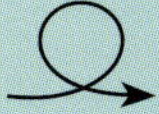

CHANGE THE POSITION

Rotate the paper 90 degrees or 180 degrees in the direction of the arrows.

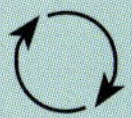

INSERT

Insert the paper in the direction of the arrow.

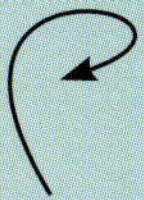

VALLEY FOLD

Fold the paper in the direction of the arrow to make a trough.

MOUNTAIN FOLD

Fold the paper in the direction of the arrow to make a peak.

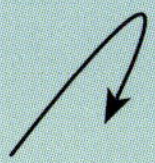

DIFFICULTY RATING

The complexity of each project in the book has been calculated on a scale of 1-3. Level 1 is the simplest, while level 3 requires the use of some complex folding techniques. If you allow yourself to gain confidence gradually you will soon be successfully creating the most intricate of designs.

INSIDE FOLD

Use this technique to surround one part of the sheet of paper with the rest, enclosing much of the fold between the outer parts of the sheet beneath the fold line.

1 Make a fold, here from corner to corner, and then turn down one corner at the intended final angle below the main crease.

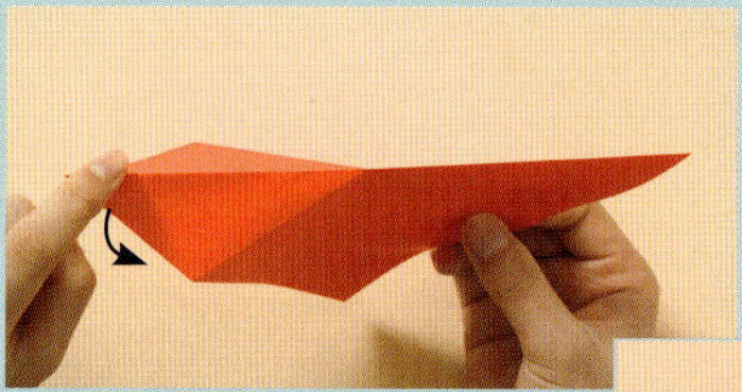

2 Lift the sheet and open out the corner that was folded over then push down the outer point of the edge, reversing the crease.

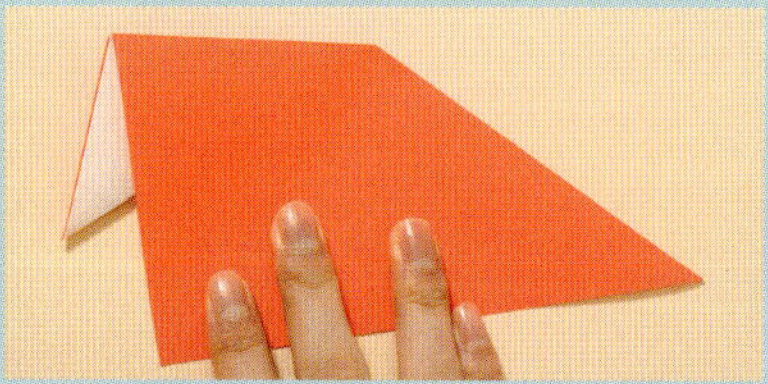

3 When the sheet is flattened the folded corner will be inside the paper with the reverse of the design showing.

OUTSIDE FOLD

Use this technique to enclose the majority of a sheet with one folded corner, pushing the folded tip over the main crease line.

1 Make a fold across the paper, turning the tip over and beyond the fold line.

2 Open out the sheet and fold the corner of the paper up and backward, reversing the creases.

3 When the sheet is flattened, the folded corner will be outside the paper with the reverse of the design showing.

CUTTING PAPER

Instead of using scissors, you can get an accurate cut with a paper cutter.

1 Mark the start and end points of your intended cut with an awl.

2 Set the metal edge of the ruler on the points marked in step 1. Cut along the ruler using the paper cutter. Be certain that the tip of the cutter follows the edge of the ruler.

SQUARE FOLD

This technique creates a square or diamond shape that can then be used as the basis for any number of origami models.

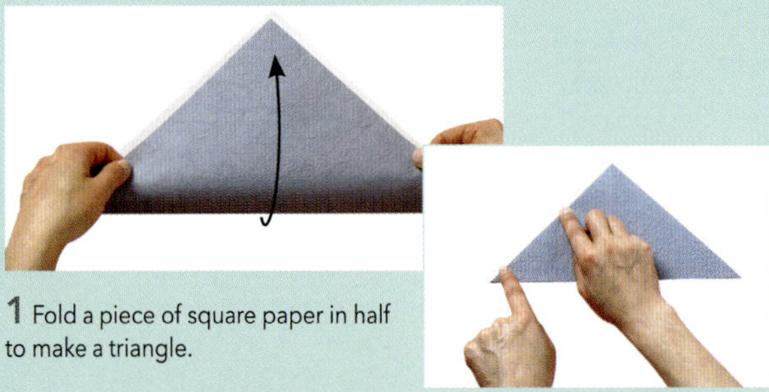

1 Fold a piece of square paper in half to make a triangle.

2 Fold it in half again.

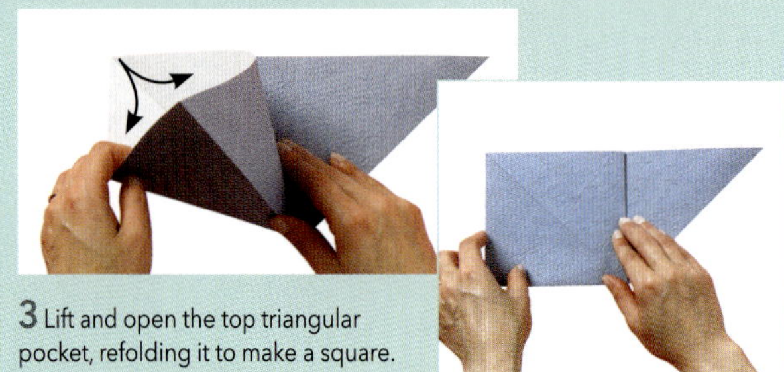

3 Lift and open the top triangular pocket, refolding it to make a square.

4 Turn the paper over and lift up the remaining triangular point.

5 Again, open out the fold and flatten it, to make a square.

TRIANGLE FOLD

In contrast, the triangle fold starts with a square shape and converts it into a triangle.

1 Fold a piece of square paper in half to make a rectangle.

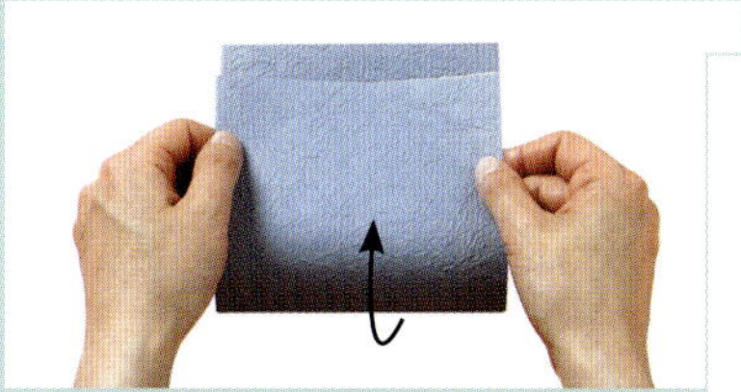

2 Fold it in half again to make a square.

3 Open out the top square pocket, refolding it to make a triangle.

4 Turn the paper over and lift the other square to the vertical.

5 Open out the square, reshaping it to make a triangle as in step 3.

01 **PENCIL** ENNPITSU

DIFFICULTY RATING:
●○○

YOU WILL NEED:
1 sheet of 6 in (15 cm) square paper
Scissors

By cutting a piece of bright paper into a long, thin rectangle you can make a fun colored pencil–any kind or size of paper will work just as well, making it a great project even if you run out of origami paper. It's perfect as a bookmark, or you can have fun decorating your school classroom or office with lots of origami pencils.

1 Cut a sheet of origami in half and fold it in half along its length to make a crease.

2 Open out the paper and turn over one end approximately ½ in (1 cm).

3 Turn the paper over and fold back the corners of the end worked on in the previous step to meet at the center crease.

4 Turn over the folded edges again, placing the angled edges together along the center line.

5 Turn the paper over and fold the flat end up so that ends up about ¾ in (2 cm) from the pointed end.

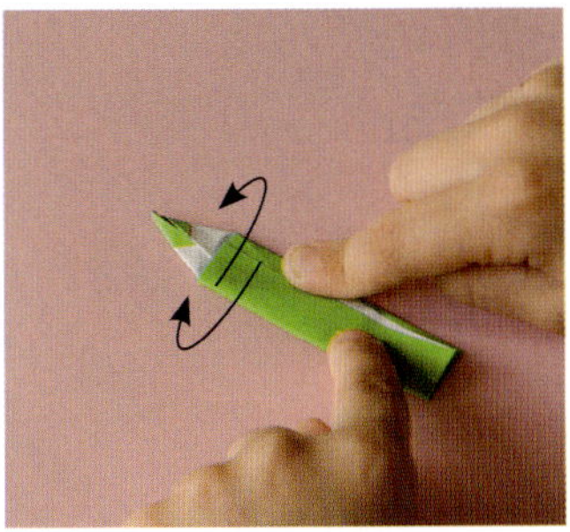

6 To finish, fold back both sides, hiding them under the object. Tuck one side into the pocket of the other so they are secure.

02 **STAR** HOSHI

DIFFICULTY RATING:

●●○

Although making a star with one piece of origami paper is simple, it can be a little fiddly at first. Like all origami, you will find it becomes much easier with a little bit of practice. You can even use paper of various sizes and patterns to make a range of colorful decorations.

YOU WILL NEED:

1 sheet of 6 in (15 cm) square paper

Drinking straw (optional)

Sticky tape (optional)

1 Start by folding the paper from corner to corner then fold in half along its longest edge.

2 Turn the upper part of the top flap forward, folding along a line across the center of the paper.

3 Fold the remaining top part of the object down and across at an angle so that the long side runs across the center of the object.

4 Lift the object and fold the top half of the object back and underneath along the center line.

5 Half open the top part of the object and pull out the flap of paper inside, reversing it as you do so.

6 Flatten it at an angle to form the next point of the star, making new creases inside the object.

7 Make a small angled flap with the bottom left-hand corner of the top layer.

8 Lift up the last remaining flap, refolding it at an angle to match the point opposite. Reverse the small fold made in the previous step to keep it in place.

9 Press down to make the last point and turn the object over. If you want, you can insert a straw into the bottom and tape it in place to make a magic wand.

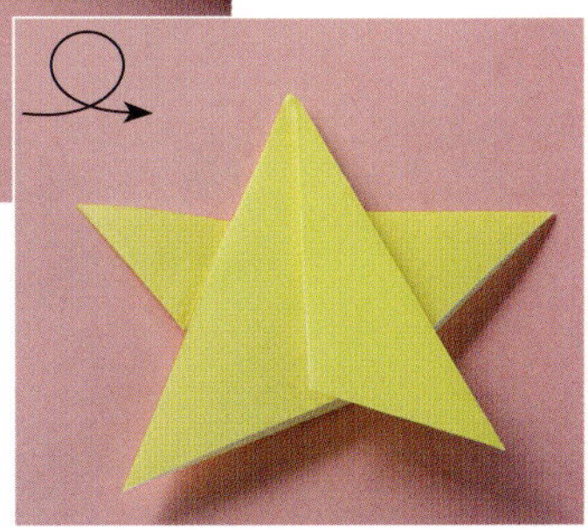

03 **AIRPLANE** HIKOUKI

DIFFICULTY RATING:

●○○

This simple glider is a cinch to make and is a brilliant flyer. With a gentle throw it will glide far and long, putting some of the more technical planes to shame. The trick is the double fold on the nose; it adds a bit of weight and helps it to go that extra bit farther.

YOU WILL NEED:

1 sheet of 6 in (15 cm) square paper

Paper glue

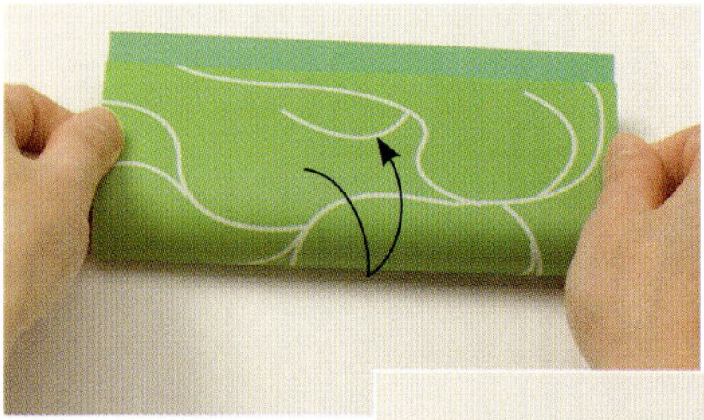

1 Fold the paper in half and open it out to make a crease then turn in the corners at one end so that they meet along the center crease.

2 Fold back the nose, making the crease about 1¼ in (3 cm) inside the folds made in the previous step then fold it back on itself, making the crease about ⅝ in (1.5 cm) from the first fold.

3 Turn the whole paper over and fold the object in half along the central crease.

4 Turn back the top wing making the fold parallel to, and approximately 1¼ in (3 cm) up from, the bottom of the plane. Turn the model over and repeat on the other side.

5 Add a dab of glue inside the body of the plane and press together to ensure the two wings sit together.

04 **GOLF CLUB** GORUF KURABE

DIFFICULTY RATING:

●○○

YOU WILL NEED:

1 sheet of 6 in (15 cm) square paper

Golf has become one of the most popular games in Japan and this origami design of a golf club allows even the smallest person to take up the game. The model is as easy to make as any in this book–as always just be careful to make sure that all the different angles are correct or you will find it rather difficult to play a good shot.

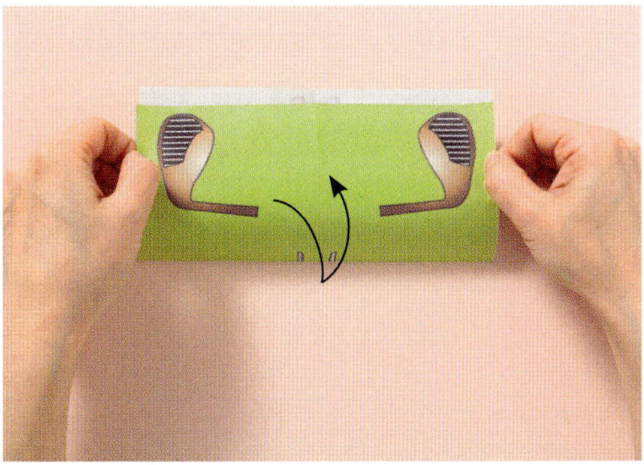

1 With the design side down, fold in half both ways to make creases, opening out each time.

2 Fold the two sides in so that they meet along the central crease.

3 Turn the paper over and then fold up the bottom edge so that it runs across the horizontal central crease.

4 Turn the paper back over and fold it in half lengthwise.

5 Pick up the paper and gently pinch the top of the creased edge of the flap. Carefully pull it down until it is at right angles to its starting point then press flat on the table.

6 Turn the left-hand side of the top flap to the left then fold the edge back over to the central crease before turning the whole flap back to the right to show the handle of the golf club. Turn the paper over and repeat on the other side.

7 Fold over the corners of the base to make a crease then refold the tips so they are inside.

05 **ORGAN** ORUGAN

This organ piano design is one of the traditional origami techniques passed down by word of mouth from generation to generation. As the technique is very simple, this project is an ideal way to learn the basics of origami—for example, how to take out a crease and open a pocket. For an added effect, I made the organ here using modern origami paper with a big check pattern.

DIFFICULTY RATING:
●○○

YOU WILL NEED:
1 sheet of 6 in (15 cm) square paper

1 Starting with the colored side down, fold the sheet in half and then into quarters.

2 Open out the last fold and bring both edges to meet in the center.

3 Open out the sides again, making triangle folds at the top.

4 Fold the central flap up to the base of the triangles and fold again along the triangles to make the keyboard.

5 Turn in the corners and let the object open out so that it sits naturally. Finally draw the black keys on to the keyboard.

06 **PACMAN** PAKU-PAKU

DIFFICULTY RATING:
●○○

YOU WILL NEED:
1 sheet of 6 in (15 cm) square paper
Googly eyes (optional)

There are many traditional origami models and this is one of the simplest. It's named after the Japanese sound effect for munching, "paku-paku." You put your fingers into the holes, and open and close the model's mouth in every different direction. You can also write a number and a word on the eight faces inside to make a fun game. Alternatively, place it upside down on a table to make a candy box you can fill with jelly beans at a party.

1 Fold the paper from corner to corner, open out and repeat in the other direction.

2 Open out and fold each of the corners into the center.

3 Turn over and fold the corners into the center once again.

4 Fold the paper in half to make a rectangle.

5 Turn over and open out by placing your fingers underneath the flaps. Finish by adding eyes if desired.

07 **HEART KITE** HART KAITE

DIFFICULTY RATING:

●●○

YOU WILL NEED:

1 sheet of 6 in (15 cm) square paper

Scissors

Sticky tape

Thread

Stapler

Drinking straw

12 in (30 cm) length of sparkling ribbon

This kite is made in the shape of a romantic heart–perhaps you could fly it as a message to a loved one–with a brilliant sparkling ribbon for the tail. Although this pretty kite is simple to make you will need to take care when cutting the paper with scissors to ensure that you create a nicely rounded heart shape. It also works as a lovely decoration to hang by a window.

1 Fold the paper in half from corner to corner to make a crease, then open it out and cut down the crease approximately 3 in (7.5 cm).

2 Turn back the two flaps at equal angles and stick them in place with sticky tape. Fold the paper in half then cut out the edge into the shape of half a heart.

3 If using the model as a working kite, tuck the thread on the inside, but if using it as a decoration, put it on the design side. Use a stapler on the design side to fix the thread in place, then tie a knot and cut off any excess.

4 Open out the model and staple one end of a straw to the widest part. Next staple the other side in place, ensuring the kite is not flat against the straw, then cut off any excess part of the straw.

5 Place the end of the ribbon at the bottom rear of the kite and staple in place.

12
3
9
6

08 **WATCH** UDEDOKEI

Wearing a watch for the first time is an important milestone for any child–being able to tell the time on your own can be a thrilling development. If a little one you know hasn't quite reached that stage yet, why not make this special origami watch so you can prepare for the real thing?

DIFFICULTY RATING:

●●○

YOU WILL NEED:

1 sheet of 6 in (15 cm) square paper

Scissors

Paper glue

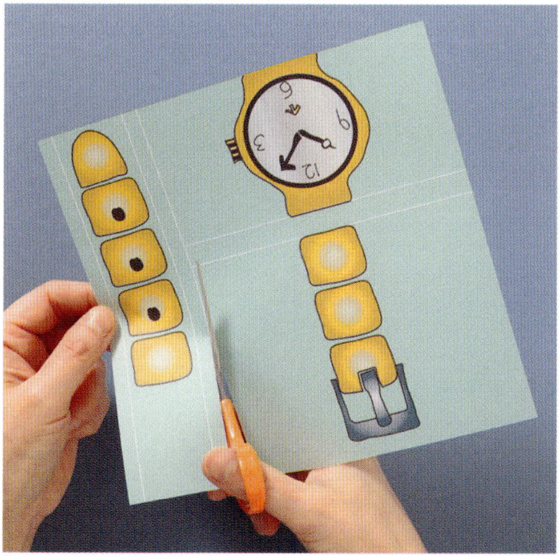

1 Use a pair of scissors to cut out the strap, using the outer line marked on the paper as a guide.

2 With the design side down, fold the remaining piece of paper in half lengthwise to make a crease then open out and fold the two long edges in so that they meet along the central crease.

3 Turn up the bottom of the paper, using the line marked on the paper as a guide, then fold it back into a concertina fold, using the marks on the paper as a guide.

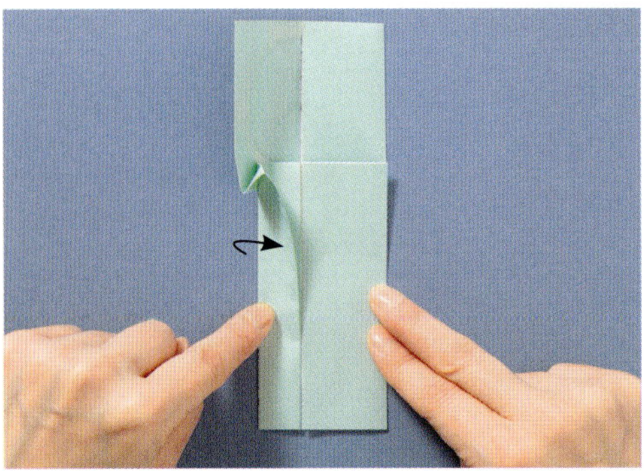

4 Carefully fold over the edges of the longer, lower section so that they meet along the center line, leaving the edges of the shorter section as they are.

5 Gently press down the edges of the folds to create new diagonal edges between the narrow and wide parts of the paper.

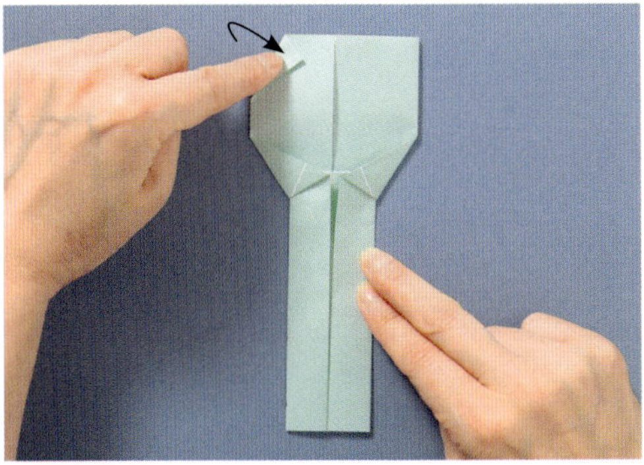

6 Fold back the top corners to make diagonal edges that mirror the creased edges made in the previous step.

7 Take the narrow piece of paper cut out in step 1 and fold over the long edges using the inner lines marked on the design as a guide.

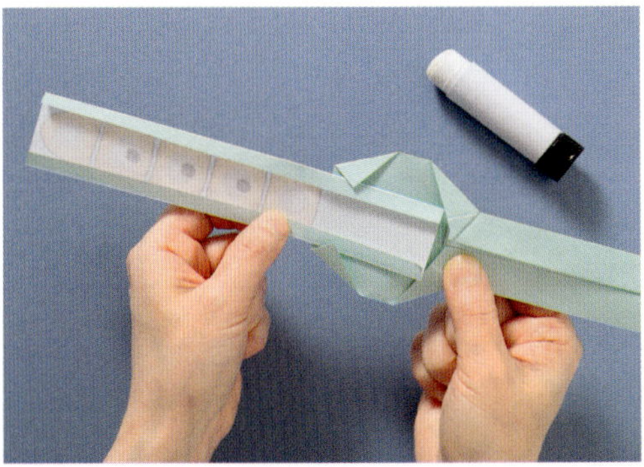

8 Put a dab of glue on one end of the strap and slide it between the last folds made on the main piece of paper then press the two together.

09 **MEDAL** KUNSHOW

DIFFICULTY RATING:

●●○

YOU WILL NEED:

1 sheet of 6 in (15 cm) square paper

Ribbon

Sticky tape

Everyone deserves a medal and now you can make your own with this simple origami design. Whether you have won the prize for baking the best cake, running the fastest race, or making the best origami model you can be proud to wear this colorful symbol of success.

1 With the design side down, fold in half both ways to make creases, opening out each time, then fold the corners into the center.

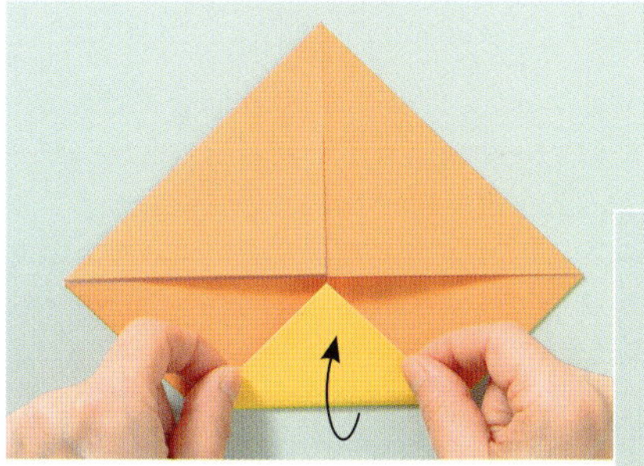

2 Fold the corners into the center again before folding the tips back to the outer edges of the paper on every side.

3 Fold back the corners now revealed in the center to run along the creased edges of the flaps.

4 Turn the paper over and fold in the corners halfway to the center point. Finish by sticking the medal on a ribbon so it can be worn.

10 **NECK TIE** NEKUTAI

DIFFICULTY RATING:
●●○

Use colorful origami paper to make a cute tie that's perfect for a Father's Day card or as part of a teddy bear's wardrobe. Alternatively, you can create a life-size tie with a sheet of paper that's 12 in (30 cm) square.

YOU WILL NEED:
1 sheet of 6 in (15 cm) square paper

1 Fold the paper from corner to corner.

2 Open out the paper and spin it 90° so that the crease is vertical. Fold the corners into the center, running the edges down the center line.

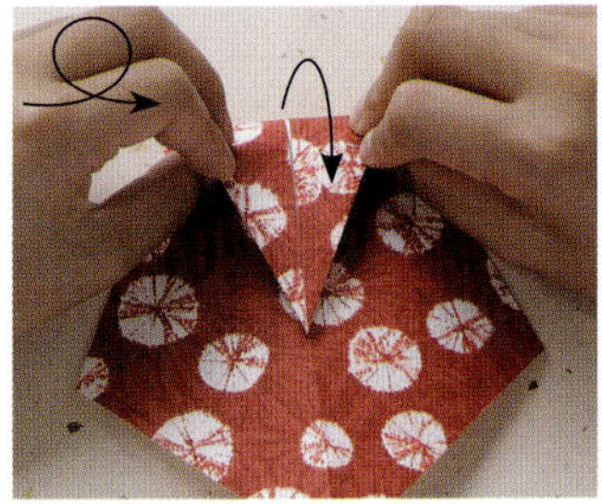

3 Turn the paper over and fold the tip forward so that it sits in line with the side points and make a crease.

4 Fold the tip back up, one-fifth of the way down from the top fold.

5 Make small folds on both sides of the long tip and push them underneath the fold made in the previous step.

6 Turn the object over and bend the tip back, halfway down its length, so that it falls on top of the main part of the object.

7 To finish, fold both sides in so that their edges meet at, and run down, the center line then turn the object over. Hook the tie over a paper collar if your teddy bear wants to wear the tie!

11 **CROWN** OU-KAN

DIFFICULTY RATING:

●●○

YOU WILL NEED:

9 sheets of 6 in (15 cm) square paper

Scissors

Paper glue

An origami crown is a party hat with a difference. You could give a gold one to the birthday girl or boy and silver versions to all your friends. Exceptionally easy to make, this design combines identically folded sheets but requires no glue or tape. I used nine sheets here, but add as many as you need to encircle the head, or use a different-sized paper. You can even use reflective paper to get that extra sparkle, like in the pictures!

1 Take one piece of paper and fold it into quarters, then open it out to leave creases. Fold the corners into the center (this is called a zabuton or floor cushion fold).

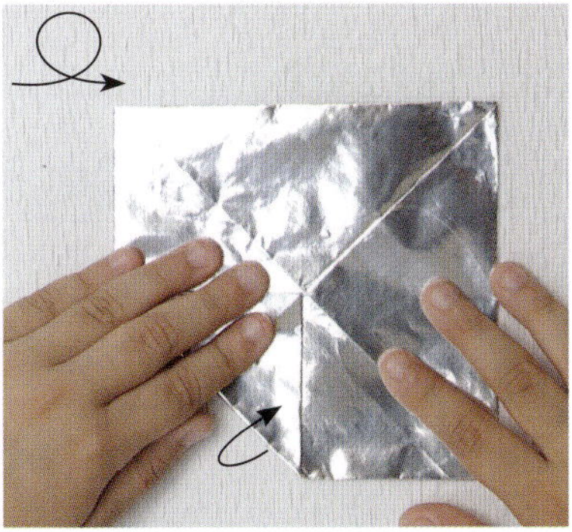

2 Turn the sheet over and fold the corner into the middle once again.

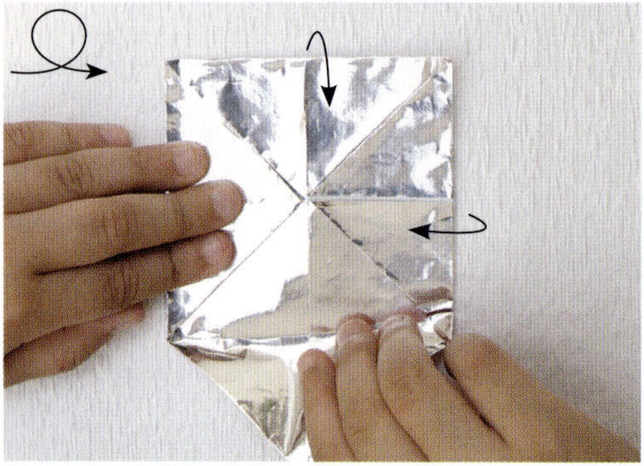

3 Turn the sheet back over and turn the corners into the middle.

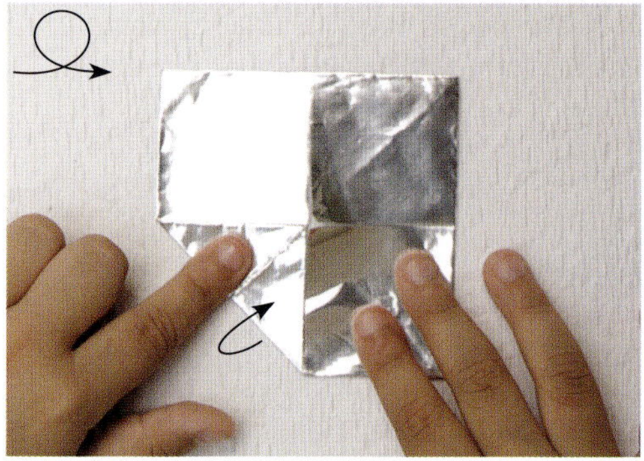

4 Turn the sheet over and again fold the corners into the center.

5 Once again, turn the sheet over and open the flaps by placing your fingers inside and pulling the paper flat. Do this to three of the four flaps.

6 Repeat steps 1-5 with the other 8 sheets of paper. When you have made all nine sections of the crown, join them together by slotting one square arm inside another. When all nine are connected close the circle by joining the two remaining ends.

12 **SPACE SUIT**
KASEI UCHUFUKU

DIFFICULTY RATING:
●●●

YOU WILL NEED:
2 sheets of 6 in (15 cm) square paper
Paper glue

To be able to travel through space, you need a lot of specialist gear. This origami space suit is much simpler to make! Some of the folds can be a bit tricky but if you follow the instructions carefully, your little astronaut will soon be taking off to explore the universe.

1 With the design side down fold the paper in half from corner to corner both ways to make creases, opening out each time, then fold the corners into the center.

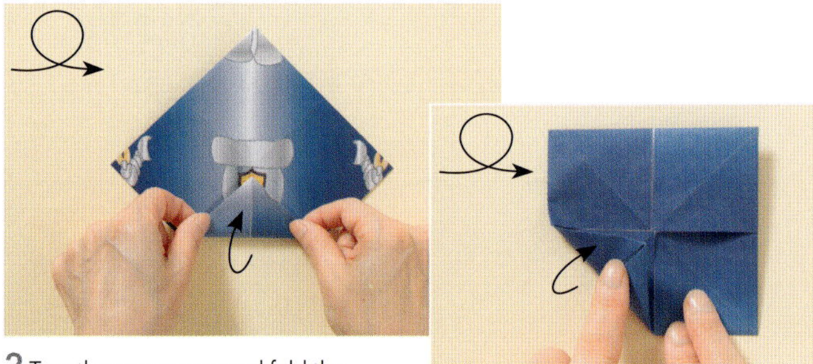

2 Turn the paper over and fold the corners into the center again then turn the paper over a second time and fold the corners into the center once more.

3 Turn the paper over again and open out the bottom flap by pulling down its top point while inserting a finger inside. Fold it flat into a square fold then repeat on both side points.

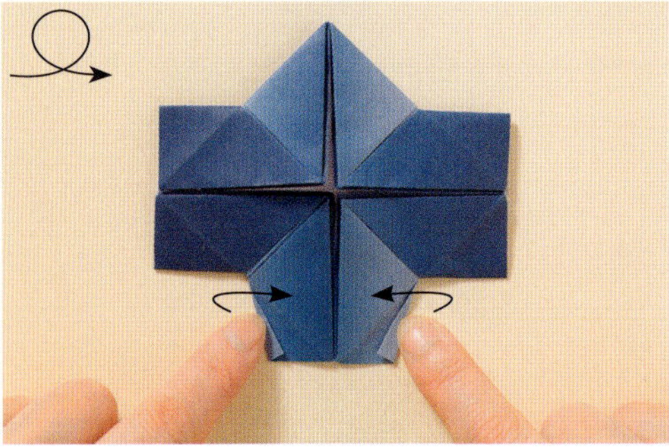

4 Turn the paper over and fold in the two bottom vertical edges at a slight angle.

5 Take the second sheet and, with the design side down, fold the paper in half from corner to corner both ways to make creases, opening out each time, then fold the corners into the center.

6 Turn the paper over and fold in the corners, then turn over again and fold in each of the corners once more, this time to make creases.

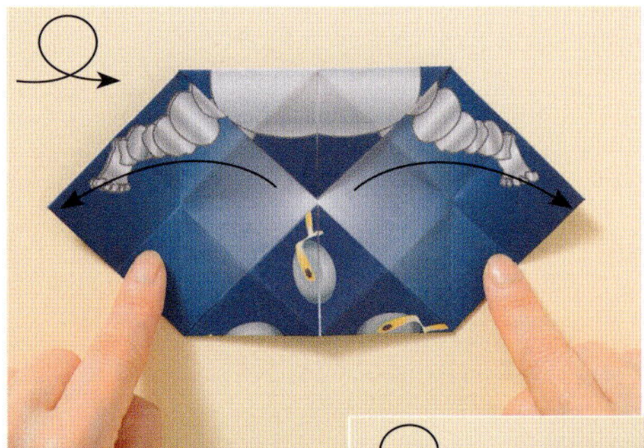

7 Open out the folds just made then turn over the paper and open out the side points. Turn the paper over again and fold over the upper diagonal edges to make creases.

8 Open out the creases just made then push the bottom left-hand point over to the middle of the model ensuring that the bottom edge now runs up the center line and the upper diagonal edge folds forward along the crease just made.

9 Turn the paper over and open out the top flap by pushing up the bottom point and opening out the two halves of the flap, refolding them into a square fold.

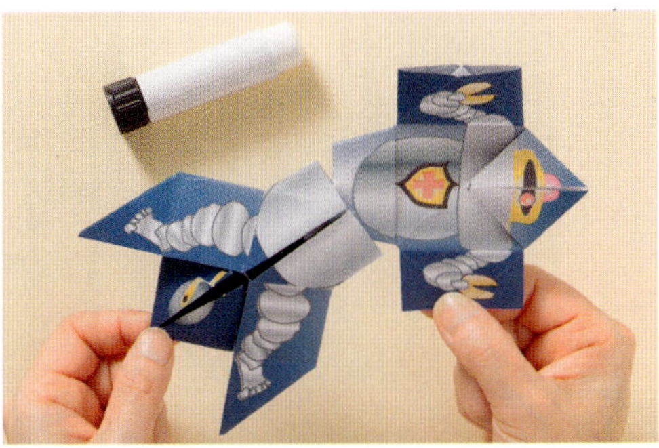

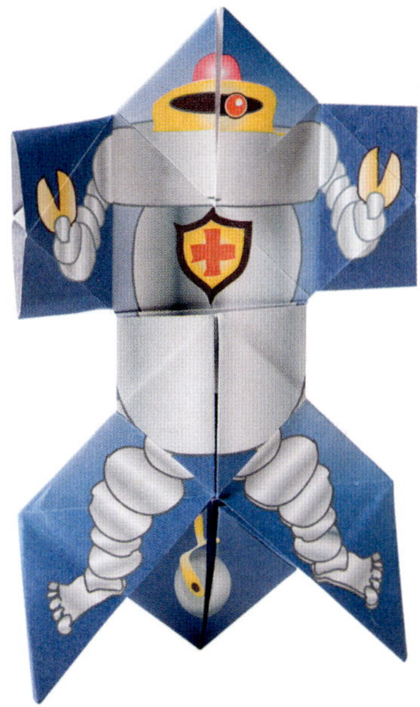

10 Take the first sheet again and cover the bottom with glue then slide it into the top of the second part of the model and press the two firmly together.

13 **WINDMILL** FUUSHA

Plant a windmill in the garden and watch it spin in the breeze, or blow into its sails and see how quickly you can make it turn. To make this origami model you will need to use both a knitting needle and scissors so it's a good idea to help any crafty little ones with those parts.

DIFFICULTY RATING:

●●○

YOU WILL NEED:

2 sheets of 6 in (15 cm) square paper

Paper glue

Knitting needle

Bendy drinking straw

Scissors

1 Take the two sheets and stick them together by placing a little paper glue in the corners and along the edges. Press together and wait for the glue to dry.

2 Fold the paper in half from corner to corner both ways to make creases, opening out each time, then fold the top and bottom points in to meet at the center point.

3 Turn the paper over and fold in the side points so that they also meet in the center.

4 Fold the bottom left and top right corners in so that they meet in the center.

5 Turn the paper over and turn in the bottom right and top left corners so that they meet in the center.

6 Open up the flap on the right-hand side that you just made and pull out the inner sheet from the center, taking it out to the left and downward, flattening it into a triangle. Repeat on the right-hand side by taking the point up and out to the right.

7 Turn the paper over and repeat with the two flaps on that side.

8 Glue under the triangular parts of the flaps on both sides to keep the model's shape.

9 Use a knitting needle to pierce a hole through the center of the paper or, if you're a young crafter, ask an adult to help you.

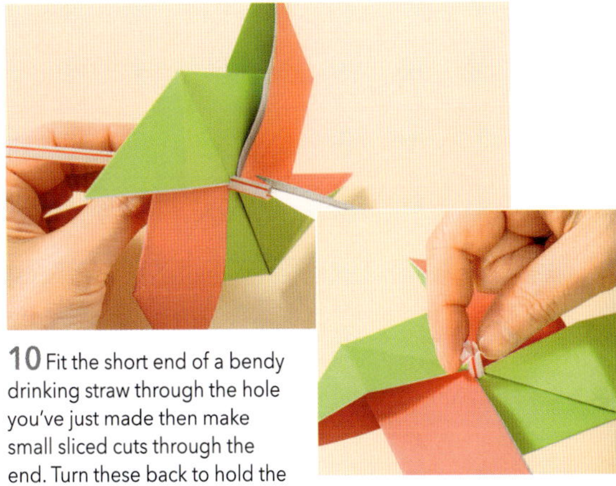

10 Fit the short end of a bendy drinking straw through the hole you've just made then make small sliced cuts through the end. Turn these back to hold the windmill in place.

11 Gently press the flaps of the windmill into shape so t hat they catch the air when you blow into them.

14 **SPINNING TOP** KOMA

Origami is magic! Here, four pieces of paper are transformed into a spinning top. Although the steps look difficult at first, they are actually unexpectedly simple. Each of the pieces of paper fits into the next until a beautifully-colored top has been created which spins around very smartly. Challenge your friends and see whose spinning top lasts the longest.

DIFFICULTY RATING:

●●●

YOU WILL NEED:

4 sheets of 6 in (15 cm) square paper

1 Fold a sheet of paper in half. Open it out, spin it 90°, and repeat before opening it out again and folding it from corner to corner.

2 Fold all of the corners to meet in the center.

3 Repeat steps 1-2 with another piece of paper. Stick the third and fourth sheets together, then repeat steps 1-2 with that piece too.

4 Spin the first piece of paper 45° and fold the corners into the center once again.

5 Repeat one more time, folding all the corners in to meet at the center.

6 Turn the object over and fold it in half in both directions to make creases from corner to corner.

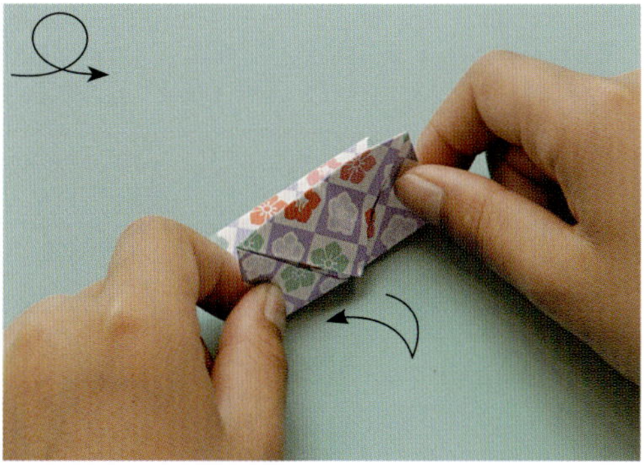

7 Next, turn the object over and fold it in half to make horizontal creases in both directions and open out.

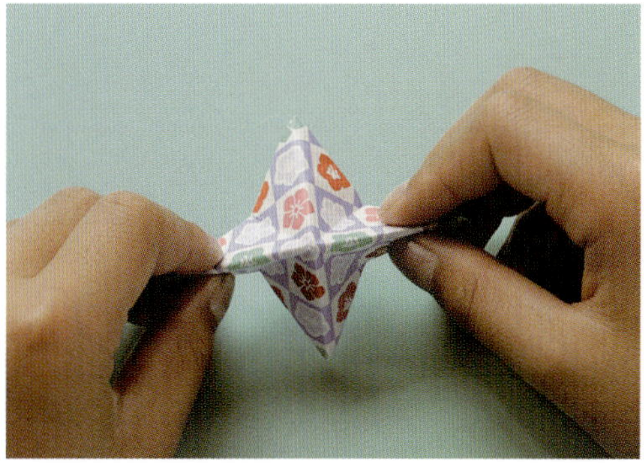

8 Squeeze the paper at the corners, pressing it together to make a point.

9 Take the second sheet, turn it over and fold the corners into the center.

10 Turn the paper over and fold the corners into the center.

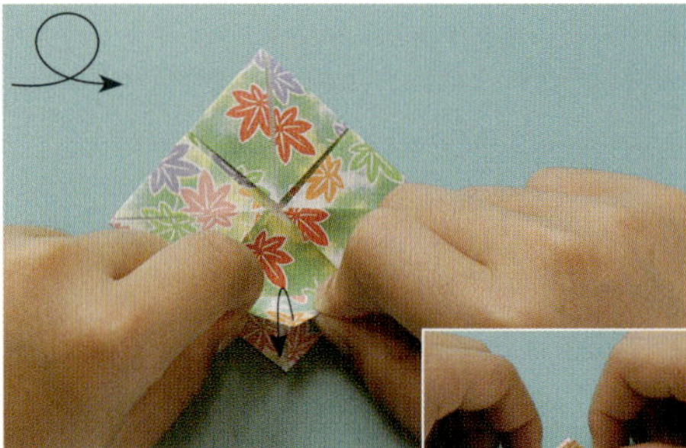

11 Turn the paper over again and fold back each of the four top flaps so that they touch the outer points.

12 Open one of the flaps on the second sheet and place one of the points of the first piec e underneath, repeating around the object until it is firmly in position.

13 Open out the third piece of paper and fold both edges into the center.

14 Spin the paper through 90° and fold both edges into the center to make the object into a square.

15 Turn back the far flap, opening out the folds to make triangles before pressing the paper flat again.

16 Repeat on the other side before turning the paper over and folding it in half toward you.

17 Fold the top left flap forward so that it points straight down.

18 Repeat, turn over, and fold forward the last two points.

19 Spin the paper 180°, pull open one flap and flatten it into a square then repeat on the other flap.

20 Turn the sheet over and repeat on the other flaps to make a rectangle.

21 Open the paper out into a square. On each of the four top flaps fold in the outer corners to meet in the middle, so that the edges run beside each other.

22 Fold each corner in, making small, equal triangles.

23 At each corner, open out the pair of flaps before folding them back over the long side of the triangles, flattening them into diamond shapes.

24 Fold back each of the four points that meet in the center to make the outline of a square.

25 Fold the long points back over the triangles toward the center.

26 Fit the first object into the this sheet, placing the corners under the flaps but on top of the folded diamonds.

15 **CARD SUITS** KARD SUTU

DIFFICULTY RATING:

●●○

Playing cards are popular all over the world and the four suits are recognizable wherever you find them. The diamonds are particularly simple and you could also use the heart as a token for someone special, but take care with the spades and clubs–they are tricky to make evenly and you also need to be careful when you glue the two parts together.

YOU WILL NEED:

5 sheets of 6 in (15 cm) square paper

Scissors

Paper glue

Diamonds

1 Cut a sheet of paper into quarters. Taking one small sheet design side down, fold it in half from corner to corner to make a crease before opening it out.

2 Fold the upper edges in to meet along the center line.

3 Fold both lower edges up to the center line in the same way to create the diamond shape.

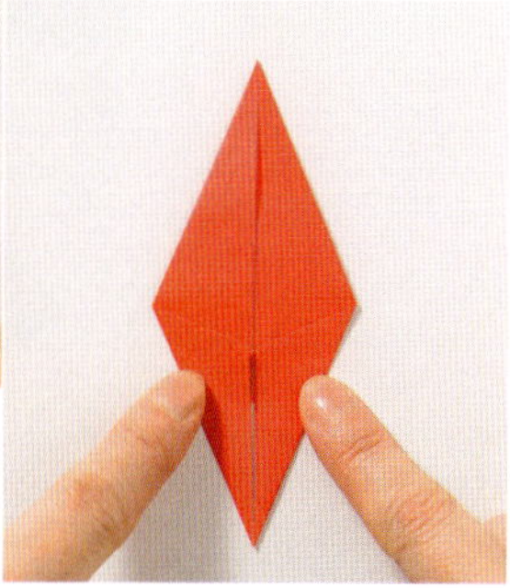

Spades

1 Take the first sheet design side down and fold it in half from corner to corner both ways, opening out each time to make creases, then turn the points in so that they all meet in the center.

2 Turn the paper over and fold the corners into the center again.

3 Fold the left-hand point into the center, allowing the single flap of paper behind to release so that the shape remains unchanged. Repeat with the top and right-hand points so that the model looks like this.

4 Turn the paper over and fold the bottom point up to the center. Finally fold the side points in to touch the vertical edges.

5 Take the second sheet and cut it into quarters. With the design side down, fold one of the small sheets from corner to corner to make a crease and open out.

6 Fold over the upper edges so that they meet along the center line then turn up the bottom point across the edges of the flaps.

7 Cover the top of this paper in glue then turn it over and push it inside the front of the first sheet, pressing all together.

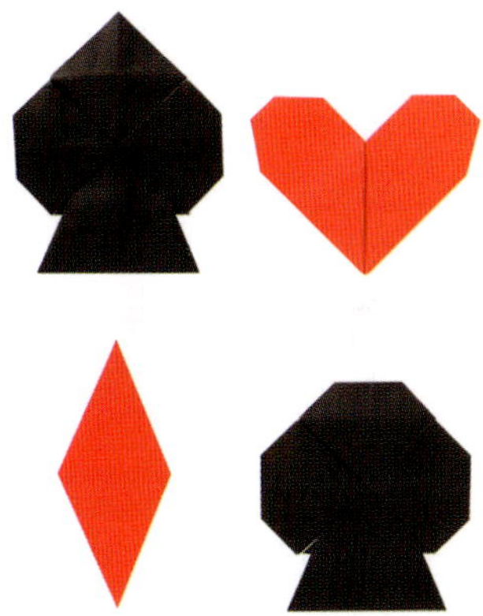

Clubs

1 To make the club suit follow exactly the same intructions as the spades until step 4. At that point also turn over the top point to touch the horizontal edge then continue as before.

2 Make the second sheet in the same way and fit the two sheets of paper together with glue as before.

Hearts

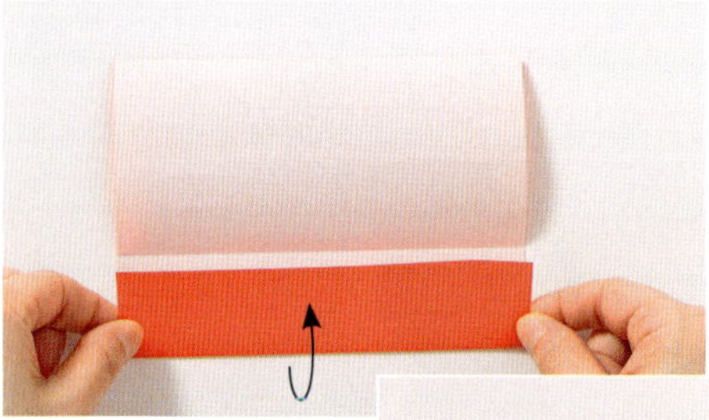

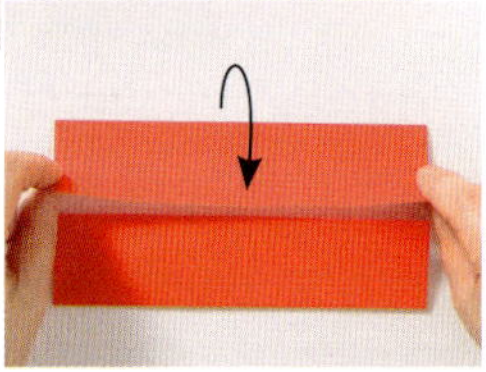

1 With the design side down, fold the sheet in half to make a crease then open out and fold the top and bottom edges in to meet along the center line.

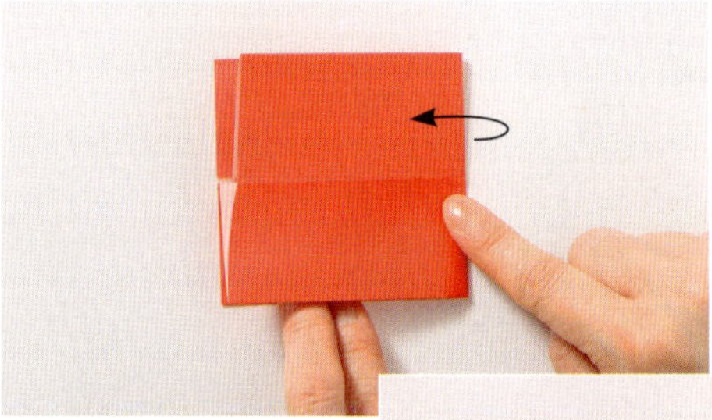

2 Fold the paper in half from side to side then again from bottom to top.

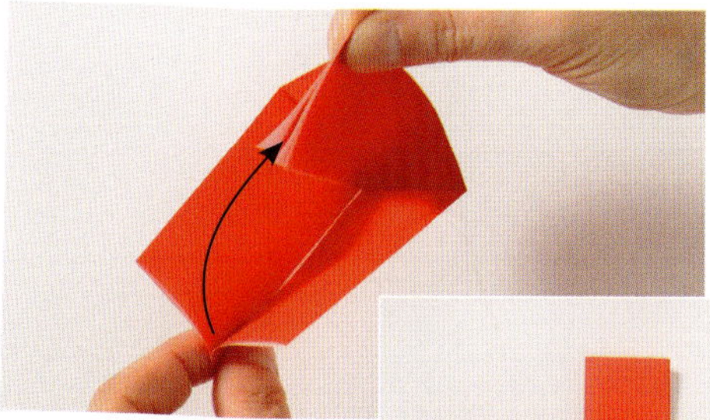

3 Holding the bottom left-hand corner, lift the paper off the table and pinch the two inner flaps, pulling them out and up until they are at right angles to their original position. Put back on the table and press flat.

4 Fold over the upper flap from the right-hand side.

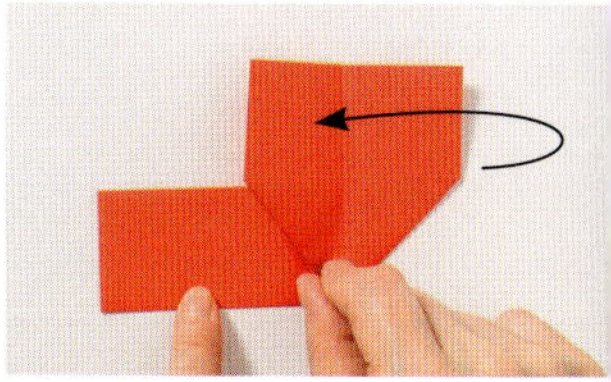

5 Turn the paper over and fold what is now the left-hand edge over to match.

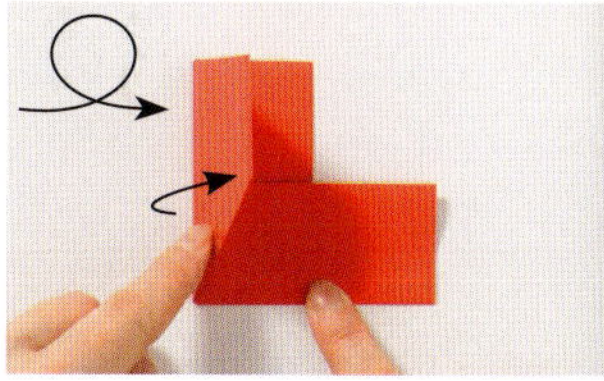

6 Spin the paper through 45° and turn over the corners of the flaps to make creases.

7 Lift the paper off the table and refold the small flaps inside the model, reversing the direction of the creases where necessary.

INDEX